SSR with Intervention

SSR with Intervention

A School Library Action
Research Project

Leslie B. Preddy

LIBRARIES
UNLIMITED

A Member of the Greenwood Publishing Group

Westport, Connecticut • London

Library of Congress Cataloging-in-Publication Data

Preddy, Leslie.
    SSR with Intervention : a school library action research project /
Leslie B. Preddy.
        p. cm.
    Includes bibliographical references and index.
    ISBN-13: 978-1-59158-460-5 (alk. paper)
    ISBN-10: 1-59158-460-4 (alk. paper)
    1. Silent reading—United States.   2. Instructional materials
centers—United States.   3. School libraries—United States.   I. Title.
    LB1050.55.P74   2007
    428.4071—dc22   2006032394

British Library Cataloguing in Publication Data is available.

Library of Congress Catalog Card Number: 2006032294
ISBN: 978-1-59158-460-5

First published in 2007

Libraries Unlimited, 88 Post Road West, Westport, CT 06881
A Member of the Greenwood Publishing Group, Inc.
www.lu.com

Printed in the United States of America

The paper used in this book complies with the
Permanent Paper Standard issued by the National
Information Standards Organization (Z39.48–1984).

10 9 8 7 6 5 4 3 2 1

For Jim—always my greatest advocate, supporter, friend.

Contents

Illustrations

FIGURES

TABLES

Preface

Does this mean I'm not stupid?
—Seventh-grade student

Oh, the love of a good read! Give me anything to read, and if it captures me emotionally or intellectually, I'm hooked for the duration. Imagine my amazement when, as a child, I learned that not everyone had the same reaction. Imagine my shock when I found that not everyone's mom carried a book in her purse 'just in case.' Imagine my horrified look when I visited friends that didn't own a bookshelf full of books. It was among these collective childhood moments that I decided I wanted to help others catch the reading bug. I felt the need to make a difference and become a book advocate.

But creating a reader isn't all that simple. I found that my love for reading wasn't enough to reach all students and staff. I needed tricks in my bag. I needed booktalks, persuasions. I became a book tease. I made videos, posters, bookmarks. I hosted book clubs and reading challenges for staff and students. But still it wasn't enough and we needed to change the attitudes of more students. If we could get them when they're young, then we could create a permanent habit.

Because of the data gathered and the positive experience of students and teachers, our action research pilot project, *Sustained Silent Reading (SSR) with Interventions* was successful in our school. It is affordable, easy to implement, takes minimal instructional planning time, and as our data prove, makes a difference in students' interest and success with reading. This book developed from our school-based action research pilot project that was implemented by a team of educators: Nancy Meyer-Brown, Dr. James Hatfield, Alison Hart, Stephanie Quinlan, Candy Schaefer, Elizabeth Sweeney, and the author, Leslie Preddy.

Proudly, we can say that our action research project, *SSR with Interventions,* was a success, and I am excited to have this opportunity to share our experience with you.

The first step toward inquiry is gaining background knowledge. Therefore, an understanding of the adolescent and adolescent readership is where we begin.

Teaching is a craft, but there is also a need to incorporate the science. This requires looking closely at educational practices, collecting data related to those practices, and responding to that data. The result of this self-analysis is purposeful instructional action based on knowledge. It is through this journey, whether the results are anticipated or not, that the educator grows as a student and continues to be educated. Chapter 2 describes our action research process, from concept inception to the concluding results. I share with you our action research journey, including how we were able to make a difference in reading attitudes, reading comprehension, and the state English/Language Arts proficiency exam.

Our inexpensive and successful instructional practice is simple to emulate. Follow the guidelines outlined in Chapter 3 to develop your own *SSR with Interventions* project in your classroom or school. It's straightforward, effective, and as the educator gains confidence with the program, enrichment ideas are suggested.

The school library media specialist is a reading motivator and reading promoter. Library media specialist support enhances and accelerates a classroom and school reading culture. Described are ideas for enhancing *SSR with Interventions* and building a reading culture.

One of the most challenging problems we had during our action research was developing generic writing prompts. This book includes prompts to be used with a group of students reading a variety of different reading material. They are organized into three sections: prompts to be used when reading material with a plot, prompts for informational text, and test readiness term prompts and definitions.

In order to simplify things, make copies of the reproducibles included for your convenience. Helpful templates include bookmarks for students and parents, home log, reading logs, and teacher logs.

Take advantage of our success and implement *SSR with Interventions* for your students. The results are so important to us that just one year later, *SSR with Interventions* is an integral piece of our School Improvement Plan and built in as part of our school day. We hope that you find the program and resources outlined here as valuable and useful to you, too.

Acknowledgments

Collaboration is a team of educators working together with a joint purpose in mind—in this case to improve the reading attitudes and test scores of our students. Collaboration is an act of faith: faith in the project, faith in the group, faith in me. This book would not have been possible without the efforts of our collaborative team: Nancy Meyer-Brown, Dr. James Hatfield, Alison Hart, Stephanie Quinlan, Candy Schaefer, and Elizabeth Sweeney. Nancy's enthusiasm as a Reading Coordinator for the district is contagious. She was a guiding light throughout the action research and the writing of this book. Without Jim, I never would have been able to analyze the data. I would still be looking at the raw data, crying hysterically I'm sure, and wondering what to do with it. And to Alison, Stephanie, Candy, and Elizabeth, you are the best and the brightest. I'm proud to have the opportunity to work with you. Thank you for your eagerness to believe in the project. Every one of you is different in your instructional style and skills, and yet all of you were willing to jump in running, because you believed in me and the instructional need. Your willingness to open your instructional practices and your heart to collaborate, eyes wide open and without pause, makes me proud to work with you.

I would also like to thank Dr. Daniel Callison. His assumption that I am capable has given me the professional confidence to try and do things I otherwise would never have attempted. I find myself working harder to prove he's right.

My ongoing gratitude goes out to Dr. Jack Humphrey. His continual efforts to advocate on behalf of adolescents, school libraries, and literacy are immeasurable. Through his efforts, Indiana politicians are not given the opportunity to forget the literacy needs of Indiana adolescents.

Introduction

Growing a reader is a task that involves the whole community. This is true for all ages, but in the adolescent years, as young people begin to cross the bridges between family life and broader community participation, diverse community contribution to their reading development becomes particularly critical.

Without the support of the entire community, adolescents will be less likely to have access to books, be encouraged to read, or be given the time to do so. Without teachers and school library media specialists who can help support the work of community agencies and public libraries, students are left to struggle on their own to gain important reading skills. Many families are not aware of their children's need for added support if they do not get information on this topic.

All adolescents need access to a variety of reading opportunities that will allow them to grow up to be successful members of a literate community. More than 70 reading stakeholders met on two different occasions to forge a blueprint for building a community of readers. These stakeholders included college reading professors, parents, principals, public librarians, school library media specialists, superintendents, teachers, and community representatives. Out of the work of this group came the following eight areas that are vital in building a community of adolescent readers.

ACCESS TO BOOKS

Access to current, appealing, high-interest, and useful books and other reading materials in their classrooms, homes, public and school libraries, and other locations within the community. Schools can ensure access to books by maintaining school library media centers with current materials. Schools need to purchase at least two books per student per year as well as to maintain adequate collections of magazines and newspapers. Many educators do not realize the extent of the decline in their school library media center books collections. Reading teachers need to support their school library media specialists and connect their students with their library media centers to ensure that the library materials are used by their students.

ENCOURAGEMENT TO VALUE READING

Schools that feature an environment where reading is valued, promoted, and encouraged. Posters and other displays that promote reading should be exhibited in classrooms and halls. School library media centers should have the resources to purchase current materials, including posters that encourage students to read. Statewide book award programs should be featured with posters and charts. School Web sites should feature reading.

TIME TO READ

Dedicated time during the school day to read for a variety of purposes—for pleasure, information, and exploration. Teachers responsible for teaching comprehension and vocabulary skills need time for both reading skill instruction and for providing the practicing of those skills through reading books, magazines, and newspapers. All teachers can be involved in Sustained Silent Reading Programs, and they can also promote independent reading that relates to their subject areas.

SKILLED READING LEADERS

Reading teachers and school library medial specialists who continually seek to renew their skills and excitement in sharing reading with students through participation in diverse professional development activities. Middle grades reading teachers should have reading licenses, just as do teachers in other subject areas. Further graduate study should lead to reading specialist licenses. The International Reading Association (IRA) is the professional organization for reading teachers, and its local and state councils offer professional development opportunities along with the IRA's publications and conferences. School library media specialists have state organizations as well as the American Library Association where conferences and publications are available.

PUBLIC LIBRARY SUPPORT

Public libraries that provide services specifically designed to engage young people's interest in reading. Most public libraries have strong collections and programs aimed at young adults. The job of school library media specialists and teachers is to help their students become users of their public libraries. Many students have never been in a public library, and they obviously do not have public library cards. Teachers and school library media specialists need to connect students with their public library programs and collections by providing field trips to the library, by arranging for visits to classrooms by public librarians, and by showing students how to access their public library opportunities using computers.

COMMUNITY AGENCY SUPPORT

Community-based programs that encourage them in all aspects of their reading development. Schools should be aware of community-based programs that are vital to their students. Many nonformal educators, even with heightened awareness, need help with program tools and ideas. Library media specialists and teachers can help connect students with youth-service programs and can assist these programs with technical assistance or training opportunities.

FAMILY SUPPORT

Opportunities for reading at home and support from schools, public libraries, and community agencies to families with adolescents to encourage family reading activities. Library media specialists and teachers can provide families with information that helps them understand the importance of their children practicing reading. Schools are not open during evenings, weekends, holidays, and summer vacation, but students can practice their reading during any of these times, if parents provide access to newspapers and obtain books and other print materials from local bookstores or public libraries.

READING ROLE MODELS

Communities of readers in which all adults—in school, at home, and across the community—serve as role models and provide guidance to ensure that reading is a priority in student's lives. Library media specialists can be very effective in helping teachers become good reading role models. They can provide a collection of current bestsellers in the library media center for teachers. Book groups can be organized by library media specialists. Older students who are good reading role models can be featured. For example, older students can promote the importance of reading during orientation sessions for younger students as they get ready to attend the school.

There is overwhelming evidence that library media centers make a difference in providing students with access to books and other print materials. Excellent school libraries are essential if we are to ensure that all adolescents have access to the reading resources that will help them to gain the level of reading achievement vital to meeting the challenge of the twenty-first century. Attention to school libraries must be at the heart of any comprehensive plan for improving adolescent reading, and library media specialists must be at the heart of a successful Sustained Silent Reading Program.

The correlation between reading achievement and voluntary reading strongly supports the need to promote and encourage adolescent voluntary reading. Independent reading accounts for one-third of a student's vocabulary growth. Students who score at the 90th percentile on reading tests read 5 times as much as children at the 50th percentile and 200 times as much as students at the 10th percentile. Schools can promote out-of-school independent reading, but not all students choose to spend their free time practicing their reading. The Sustained Silent Reading Program ensures that all students are at least spending some time reading materials of their choice, and as students find interesting materials to read during the program, they naturally continue to read such materials away from school.

This book outlines how to inaugurate a Sustained Silent Reading Program. It is important to have such a guide to ensure that the Sustained Silent Reading Program is sustained in the school. Schools are quick to adopt this and that for their schools, but without proper planning such programs often do not last very long.

All teachers in a school believe the content they teach is important. They are thus reluctant to provide time for a Sustained Silent Reading Program. They need to be involved in the planning and implementation of the program and be provided with appropriate evaluation information so that they see that the program is valuable for them and their students.

Any program will become less productive over time without support and continued upgrading. The students change from year to year, but the faculty is more constant. They need to know that the school will provide access to appropriate reading materials and that their efforts are recognized.

I have visited Perry Meridian Middle School and worked with reading teachers and their library media specialist, Leslie Preddy. The principal and faculty are all supportive of the program, but it would not exist without the interest and leadership of the library media specialist. This is a program that will improve reading for all students, providing that it is properly implemented. Be careful in the way you begin such a program, plan well, study the work presented in the book, and develop a successful and lasting Sustained Silent Reading Program for your students.

Jack Humphrey
Middle Grades Reading Network
University of Evansville
jh25@evansville.edu
http://mgrn.evansville.edu

1

The Adolescent and Reading

She was helping people become whoever it was they were going to turn
out to be. Because when you read a book as a child it becomes part of
your identity in a way that no other reading in your whole life does.

—Meg Ryan as children's bookseller Kathleen Kelly in *You've Got Mail* (1998)

Middle school students can be a tough crowd. They have so many emotions, people, gadgets, and activities pulling at their attention, it's hard to gain their awareness, and sometimes it seems nearly impossible to get them excited about something as unpopular to an adolescent as reading. Even in those die-hard reading fans who enter my library media center every week, I'd be hard-pressed to find one who would openly admit to a group of peers that he likes to read. In this harsh climate, how is it possible to establish a school climate for readers? First, one must understand the beast that is the adolescent.

BRAIN DEVELOPMENT

Fight brain decay—Read! The key to learning is investment and engagement. Brain-compatible instruction includes a focus on developing a student's ability to use information, actively constructing meaning, focusing on authentic tasks, teaching only one thing at a time, and establishing a nonthreatening environment for students (McGann 2003). Students need reading practice. The student needs to read, think about what he read, discuss what he read, and know that the educator is not judging him throughout the process.

The Adolescent Brain

Pat Wolfe (2003) explains that to think is to activate an entire network of neurons. If something has no meaning, the brain has trouble holding on to it, so reading for meaning is important, especially with adolescents still developing their skills as readers. Developing readers need help through modeling, reading for a purpose, activating prior knowledge, and communication. The brain also needs to connect emotionally, so it is helpful for students to have an emotional connection to reading and to feel that the educator relates to them emotionally. Conversely, forcing a nonreader to read books in which he has no interest, instead of allowing free choice—or at least choices related to personal interests—will equate reading in that student's mind to a negative, a punishment. If reading has an emotional, or motivational, impact, the reading and the skill to read is remembered longer. Emotional development is the foundation to cognitive development. Brain functionality does not reach capacity until an individual is about 21–24 years old.

Using a part of the brain for something, such as reading, increases the brain's ability for that specific thing. Students need to continually be actively engaged in positive reading experiences. Practicing something, such as reading, makes permanent connections in the brain. When a person uses a part of the brain for something, he increases the brain's ability for that specific skill, which Wolfe calls a definite "use it or lose it" (Wolfe 2003).

The Adolescent and Emotions

According to brain research, the brain has reached adult size by adolescence, but the brain during the teen years is going through complex changes and developing at a rate comparable to that of a toddler, which many adults call the "terrible-twos." The brain is not fully developed until 18 to 20 years of age. Pat Wolfe (handout, 2003) states that adolescent behavior is "characterized by swings of mood, risk taking, poor judgment, disorganization, disrespect for authority, and little emotional control," which researchers suspect is correlated to brain development occurring during adolescence. The adolescent is hardwired to respond emotionally, without any intellectual thought. The student reacts first, is rational last. The prefrontal lobes, responsible for things such as decision making, planning, and focusing, is the last to work efficiently, making them inefficient, whereas the amygdala—the part of the brain responsible for emotions and emotional memory—is already fully formed. This helps explain adolescents' sometimes extreme and irrational behavior and reactions to situations. Because of the nature of the adolescent brain, adolescents have difficulty correctly interpreting the emotions of others, don't relate to other's emotions or situations well, and don't read facial expressions effectively (Wolfe 2003).

READING = SUCCESS

A 2004 report from the National Endowment for the Arts, "Reading at Risk: A Survey of Literary Reading in America," states that literary reading is dropping (National Endowment for the Arts [NEA] 2004). From 1982 to 1992 young adults (ages 18–24) mark the sharpest decline in literary reading. It concludes that there is a correlation between reading literature for pleasure and higher education and income level, urban residency, gender (female), and ethnicity and race (white American). So, in a sense, a greater tendency toward a habit of reading can mean a better potential life income.

According to "Reading between the Lines: What the ACT Reveals about College Readiness in Reading," a report based on the 2005 ACT test, a developed literacy in reading is an essential, determining factor for entry-level workplace and college (trade, technical, 2-year, 4-year) readiness and success (ACT 2006). Students seem to agree. Results reported in *School Library Journal* ("Poll Says" 2001) of a poll conducted for the National Education Association finds secondary students agreeing that reading skills equal life success. The ACT Executive Summary (2006) states, "Not enough high school teachers are teaching reading skills or strategies and many students are victims of teacher's low expectations" (p. 4). If we expect a student to reach his adult potential, a fully-developed habit of reading is needed.

The School Library Media Center

Students need free and open access to currently popular pleasure reading material, both fiction and nonfiction. In Indiana, through the leadership efforts of Dr. Jack Humphrey and the Middle Grades Reading Network, the Indiana General Assembly provided extra funding from 1997 to 2003 through the Printed Materials Grant to provide pleasure reading materials for school library media centers (Holland and Humphrey 2004). Indiana University's Indiana Education Policy Center report concluded that "the library materials program appears to be associated with a number of positive student outcomes, including increased use of library materials, increased student ownership of school libraries, higher levels of independent reading, and higher reading achievement" (Plucker et al., 2002, p. 18).

Sixteen different state studies, beginning in 1992 with the first Colorado Study, find a positive relationship between the school library media program and student achievement. Conclusions of these studies are that students in schools with an effective library media center run by a qualified school library media specialist have higher levels of achievement than students in schools without library media centers (Lance 2003; *School Libraries Work!* 2006). A library media center provides access to a wide variety of reading materials in a variety of formats and topics, which is integral to reading success. *Libraries and Reading: Indispensable Partners* (1996) explains that a library media center is important to developing readers and that library media centers should contain a wide range of up-to-date reading material that is appealing in appearance, written at a variety of reading levels (ranging from below grade to challenging text), offer comfort reading (popular interests, authors, etc.), and unfamiliar reading (unfamiliar topics, authors, etc.).

Sustained Silent Reading

Free Voluntary Reading (FVR) is a term used by Stephen Krashen (2004) that encompasses a variety of in-school student choice reading programs, including Sustained Silent Reading (SSR). The foundation of SSR is the classroom teacher and all other adults in the school and students reading simultaneously. Furthermore, students require choice in what they read (Smith and Wilhelm 2002; Krashen 2004). According to Krashen's review of the research spanning nearly a century, free reading has a positive impact on grammatical development, reading comprehension, spelling, vocabulary, and writing style and is equal to or better than "direct (traditional) instruction" for grammar, reading, vocabulary, and writing. SSR also helps build stamina, the reader's ability to read and stay focused on the reading for a length of time (Burke 2000).

THE MIDDLE SCHOOL READER

There are three types of adolescent readers: effective, apathetic and reluctant, and resistive and struggling. All students need time and opportunity to build successful relationships with reading material and reading role models, including peers, educators, parents, and caregivers.

In a position statement released by the International Reading Association (Moore et al. 1999), adolescent reading achievement is correlated to reading attitudes, effective literacy instruction, and access to reading opportunities and reading material. The report emphasizes the importance for schools to provide time for students to read material of student choice. Schools must also provide necessary support in the form of materials availability, reading conversations, and educators modeling effective reading strategies and promoting reading. The report states that:

> Time spent reading is related to reading success.
> Time spent reading is associated with attitudes toward additional reading.
> Time spent reading is tied to knowledge of the world.
> Reading is a worthwhile life experience (p. 5).

The Resistive and Struggling Reader

The resistive and struggling reader is reading below grade level, does not have the skills necessary to effectively decode reading material, considers reading a chore worth avoiding, and has feelings of ineffectiveness that are often expressed through aggression, disruptions, and attempts to distract others and himself (Curtis and Longo 1999). Kay Bishop (2003) shares characteristics that might be visible in a resistive reader, but warns that a resistive reader may not exhibit all of the characteristics.

Reading below Grade Level

A resistive and struggling reader does not have the skills necessary to read effectively at grade level.

Weak Home Library

The family has a limited home library with very few books, magazines, or newspapers. There may not be a reading role model in the home.

Peer Isolation

The student may have difficulty relating appropriately to fellow students. He might be the student last chosen for a group, may be estranged from his peers, and may not fit in socially. He may be boisterous, act out, use exaggerated mannerisms; or he may be the extreme opposite, avoiding attention from educators and peers.

One-Dimensional Reader

A resistive or struggling reader is, as Bishop states, "interested in only certain types of reading material" (p. 70). This could be in format, formula, or theme. This may be the student who wants to read only a particular series, or only material by a particular author, or only books about a particular thing—like a favorite sport—or in a particular format—like a Web site or a graphic novel.

Television

A resistive or struggling reader watches a lot of television. Television time may be used as a babysitter, friend, time-filler, constant background noise, or as a substitute for social interaction.

Laura Robb (2005) goes further to describe ways that an educator can create "struggling readers." She lists six ways an educator can encourage a resistive and struggling reader to continue to resist and struggle:

> work in text that is too hard for a student;
> complete skills worksheets instead of logging "reading mileage";
> students reading aloud for no real purpose (i.e., round-robin);
> limit the amount of meaningful discussion students have related to their reading;
> substitute reading aloud for students reading the material;
> make the focus of reading answering a series of factual questions.

The resistive and struggling reader needs survival skills for managing texts, training on effective reading strategies, and a variety of modeling experiences with effective adult and peer readers. These students need to read with a purpose (Tovani 2005). For a student to read with a purpose, he needs a clear understanding of why he is reading, for what information he should be looking, and how to look for what is important in his reading. This purpose can be developed through pre-reading discussion or reading with a question, or prompt, in mind. After reading, the student writes a response to the question, which allows the student to narrow focus while reading.

The Apathetic and Reluctant Reader

An apathetic adolescent reader is aliterate. He can read at or above grade level, but prefers not to read. If given a choice, this student would not choose to read. In most cases, it would not even occur to him to list reading as a choice. This student needs help changing attitudes about reading. To become an effective reader, the apathetic reader needs choice, a variety of reading material nearby, a change in attitude, and modeling experiences that encourage the traits of an effective reader.

The Effective Reader

The effective reader is literate. Jean Donham (1998) describes literacy as "the ability to gain information or vicarious experience from reading" (p. 143). An effective reader knows how to release his time and place and lose himself in the world of images liberated in his mind by the text. What is known about effective adult readers can also be applied to the adolescent. According to Steve Gardiner (2005), there are six traits of a "good adult reader." Just as in an effective adult reader, these traits can be applied to characteristics educators and parents attempt to develop and encourage in children. Not all traits will be seen or absorbed by all readers, but an effective reader will have some of these traits.

Multiple Books

An effective reader may choose to read more than one book at a time. Why? The reader has a variety of interests and purposes for reading going at the same time: information, instruction, and entertainment. Proximity to the reading material may also play a factor. I noticed this trait in my own son, a mid-year third grader at the time, and asked him why he reads more than one book at a time and his response was that he feels the reading moves faster that way and he likes leaving books different places (car, school, home) so that there is one nearby. So then I asked him how he keeps track of what is going on in the different books and he answered, "You know, I just hold the book and go through my memory about it, then, you know, I start reading and it takes me to, like, this other dimension."

Rereading

An effective reader considers rereading informative or enjoyable material a worthwhile activity. A good reader sees that every time he reads a beloved piece, he finds something new he hadn't realized before. It takes him back to re-experience something remembered fondly, like knowing that when you visit Grandma, you'll get to taste her delicious cookies. This reader knows that going back to reread something enjoyed before, no matter the format, genre, or purpose, has a sense of familiarity and security. It's not knowing what will happen next that is important, but the journey taken to get there.

Keep Reading Materials Nearby

A good reader plans ahead. This reader often keeps something to read on hand for those occasions when a wait is expected or unexpectedly necessary. These students may have a book or magazine in their sports bag, ready to read if a ride is late. You might be able to catch them occasionally reading on the bus or while traveling long distances. An effective reader may have reading material handy while waiting for an appointment or other activity where he knows he'll probably have a wait.

Knowing When to Give Up

This is one time that not finishing an activity is okay. Where did the myth get established that if a person starts a book, he must finish it? Absolutely not! An effective reading skill is realizing when the reading is not enjoyable or productive. A good reader may give the author an appropriate amount of reading, maybe a few chapters of a book, to capture the reader's attention and make that reading worth the time and effort. If the author has not properly established interest or purpose in that time, an effective reader may decide to set the reading material aside. At a later time, sometimes just a week or a few months later, other times not for years, the reader may give the author another chance, but other times not.

Sharing/Not Sharing

Sometimes a good reader enjoys sharing what he's read or is reading with others. He may want to tell others what he learned or encourage others to experience the emotional or engaging moments of the story. Other times the reading may be so personal and reflective that he finds pleasure in internalizing the occasion and keeping it to himself.

Freedom of Choice

Freedom is a staple of American history and culture. Americans are raised on the freedoms our Bill of Right affords and it carries over into everyday life, beliefs, and feelings. People like to choose what to do. Interested in listening to a group of adults complain the loudest? Take away some freedoms, some choice. The same can be said for kids, especially adolescents. Students want to have some authority and control in their lives. This includes sovereignty for what a student spends his time reading.

To Gardiner's six traits, add three more traits of an effective reader. Included in a lifelong reader's traits are losing oneself in the text, format adaptability, and home bookshelves.

Losing Oneself

A good reader might sometimes become obsessively absorbed in the reading. This happens when the characters, events, and descriptions become so real the reader continues to think about them when not reading. The reader becomes so absorbed he allows himself to be taken inward to the alternate reality established by the relationship between the reader's imagination and the text. When not reading, the reader is preoccupied and can't stop thinking about the reading. The material becomes so absorbing in that moment, while reading, the reader forgets his own time and place.

Format

Literacy comes in many forms and for many purposes. Reading can be found on a cereal box, Web site, food label, manual, instructions, job application, graphic novel, newspaper, bookmark, brochure, mail, novel, nonfiction, textbook—and the list goes on. An effective reader understands that reading comes in a variety of formats and that there are different literacy skills necessary to manage and manipulate information, depending on the format. A good reader is able to cope with many, but not necessarily all, formats intuitively, or with minimal conscious thought.

Home Bookshelf

A home that promotes, supports, and discusses reading and reading material has a positive impact on reading achievement (Milam 2003). An effective reader has a home with books and other reading material. This includes family members visibly reading frequently and supporting readership. To develop a lifelong reader, a person who makes the conscious choice to read, a culture of home libraries must be established. Students with home libraries see reading as a free time choice and something that can be done outside of the school.

THE SCHOOL CULTURE AND CLIMATE

A school that cultivates a lifelong love of reading and readership has developed an island universe where all hearts are engaged in reading, where reading is given the status of sports in the school, and where weak and immature readers are given the necessary time and attention to alter their perceptions and success. To cultivate successful readers, a school must extend reading and reading strategies into every classroom and content area (McKenzie 2005).

The Influence of a Good Teacher

"Engaged readers are socially interactive" (Dreher 2003, p. 338). Teachers need to be one of those engaged readers. When a reader finds moving literature, he has the urge to share that emotion. A reader exploring informational text that alters his known universe feels the need to share what has been learned. A reader who experiences an epiphany through a reading experience desires to share. Being an engaged reader means wanting to share the experience. Donham (1998) explains, "Enthusiasm for reading among teachers provides an important role model for students … creating among teaching staff a community of readers can be a major contribution to creating a community of readers among students" (p. 150). This is reinforced by Dreher, "In short, teachers who are engaged readers are motivated to read, are both strategic and knowledgeable readers, and are socially interactive about what they read. These qualities show up in their classroom interactions and help create students who are, in turn, engaged readers" (p. 338).

The Influence of a Good Library Media Specialist

The school library media specialist has an impact on the culture and climate of reading in the school. The library media specialist plays an integral role in literacy development, teacher training, student motivation, and parent involvement. She models and teaches students and teachers strategies for effective reading and writing, and is strongly involved in reading promotion (Haycock 1999). Keith Curry Lance's research on school libraries in various states finds that an aspect of staff activities included in effective library media programs, which are predictors of academic achievement, is "motivating students to read" (Power Point, 2003). The library media specialist promotes reading through book selection and collection development; establishing a warm and welcoming library media center with access to a wide variety of books; advocating schoolwide reading, reading aloud, and booktalks; supporting book and reading clubs; communicating to parents; and other strategies necessary to maintain reading momentum (Zimmerman 2005).

Collaboration

Collaboration between the classroom teacher(s) and the library media specialist requires trust, respect, and a supportive administration to be a successful partnership of thinking, planning, and implementation. The library media specialist takes on a "persistent" and "proactive" leadership role in developing collaborations and relationships with administrators, classroom teachers, and students (Bishop 2003, p. 8). One study found that it was more successful to develop a reading program through collaboration than through a computerized reading program, such as Accelerated Reader or Reading Counts. Further, the collaboration has an even greater impact on reading skill and motivation if reading motivation strategies are incorporated into the reading program developed by the collaboration (Haycock 2005).

Routine

In a study conducted at the Boys Town Reading Center, reading problems in adolescents were examined (Curtis and Longo 1999). The study found that struggling readers require the structure of routine. The students need materials in a convenient location, and their willingness to participate hinges upon a clear understanding of the educator's expectations and what the student will be expected to do: how, when, where, why. A student may occasionally huff and complain about the repetition of routine, but it's mostly hot air. The students rely upon the stability and consistency of habitual routine.

Attitude

Teaching positive reading attitudes is just as important as teaching effective reading strategies. Attitude-changing behavior includes reading aloud, communicating about books, and giving books to kids (Bishop 2003; Haycock 2005). One study confirms the connection between a school with a library media specialist and students' positive attitudes about reading (Ontario Library Association 2006). Instilling a positive attitude about reading is more than half the battle toward developing a lifelong reader. The external motivation derived from a school creating a culture and climate of reading helps students develop their intrinsic desires to read.

A study about Accelerated Reader (Everhart 2005) that can apply to other reading situations concluded that boys are motivated to read through prizes, praise, and recognition whereas girls are motivated to read through social reading: reading with others and book discussion. This emphasizes the different motivation tactics needed to influence both genders. A school's effective reading promotion plan incorporates promotion styles necessary for impacting boys and girls.

REFERENCES

ACT. "Reading between the Lines: What the ACT Reveals about College Readiness in Reading." 2006. http://www.act.org/path/policy/reports/reading.html. (Accessed 6 June 2006).

Bishop, Kay. *Connecting Libraries with Classrooms: The Curricular Roles of the Media Specialist.* Washington, OH: Linworth, 2003.

Burke, Jim. *Reading Reminders: Tools, Tips, and Techniques.* Portsmouth, NH: Heinemann, 2000.

Curtis, Mary E., and Ann Marie Longo. *When Adolescents Can't Read: Methods and Materials That Work.* Newton, MA: Brookline Books, 1999.

Donham, Jean. *Enhancing Teaching and Learning: A Leadership Guide for School Library Media Specialists.* New York: Neal-Schuman, 1998.

Dreher, Mariam Jean. "Motivating Teachers to Read." *The Reading Teacher* 56 (4): 338–340 (2002/2003).

Everhart, Nancy. "Accelerated Reader." American Library Association. 2005. http://www.ala.org/ala/aasl/aaslpubsandjournals/slmrb/slmrcontents/volume82005/reader.htm. (Accessed 6 February 2006).

Gardiner, Steve. "A Skill for Life." *Educational Leadership* 63 (2): 67–70 (2005).

Haycock, Ken. "Collaborative Literature-Based Reading Programs with Motivation Components." *Teacher Librarian* 33 (2): 38 (2005).

————. *Foundations for Effective School Library Media Program.* Englewood, CO: Libraries Unlimited, 1999.

Holland, Earlene, and Jack W. Humphrey. "Study of Reading in Indiana Middle, Junior, and Senior High Schools." Middle Grades Reading Network. March 2004. http://mgrn. evansville.edu/study2004.htm. (Accessed 25 March 2006).

Krashen, Stephen. *The Power of Reading: Insights from the Research.* 2d ed. Westport, CT: Libraries Unlimited, 2004.

Lance, Keith Curry. "Powering Achievement: The Latest Evidence on How School Libraries Matter to Academic Achievement." Presentation at American Association of School Librarians Annual Conference, Kansas City, MO, October 2003.

Libraries and Reading: Indispensable Partners. Evansville, IN: Middle Grades Reading Network, 1996.

McGann, Mary. "Brain Matters Preview." Workshop presentation at Metropolitan School District of Perry Township Professional Development Seminar, Indianapolis, IN, May 2003.

McKenzie, Jamie. "Power Reading and the School Library." *Library Media Connection* 23 (5): 14–19 (2005).

Milam, Peggy. "Scientifically Based Reading Research: Implications for Instruction." *School Library Media Activities Monthly* 20 (2): 20–22, 26 (2003).

Moore, David W., et al. "Adolescent Literacy: A Position Paper for the Commission on Adolescent Literacy of the International Reading Association." International Reading Association. 1999. http://www.reading.org/downloads/positions/ps1036_adolescent. pdf. (Accessed 1 June 2006).

National Endowment for the Arts. "Reading at Risk: A Survey of Literary Reading in America." Research Division Report #46. 2004. http://www.nea.gov/pub/ReadingAtRisk.pdf. (Accessed 1 June 2006).

Ontario Library Association. "School Libraries & Student Achievement in Ontario." 2006. http://www.accessola.com/osla/graphics/eqao_pfe_study_2006.pdf. (Accessed 1 June 2006).

Plucker, Jonathan A., et al. *Improving School Libraries and Independent Reading: 1997–2002 Impact Evaluation of the K-12 School Library Printed Materials Grant.* Policy Issue Report #2002–02. Bloomington: Indiana University-Indiana Education Policy Center, 2002.

"Poll Says Most Teens Value Reading." *School Library Journal* 47 (8): 16 (2001).

Research Foundation Paper: School Libraries Work! 2006 ed. Danbury, CT: Scholastic Library Publishing. 2006. http://www.scholastic.com/librarians/printables/downloads/slw_2006.pdf. (Accessed 6 December 2006).

Robb, Laura. "Reading Strategies That Work." Presentation at the Adolescent Literacy Conference. Indianapolis, IN, June 2005.

Smith, Michael W., and Jeffrey D. Wilhelm. *"Reading Don't Fix No Chevys": Literacy in the Lives of Young Men.* Portsmouth, NH: Heinemann, 2002.

Tovani, Cris. "The Power of Purposeful Reading." *Educational Leadership* 63 (2): 48–51 (2005).

Wolfe, Patricia. "Brain Matters: Translating Research into Classroom Practice." Workshop presentation at Metropolitan School District of Perry Township Professional Development Seminar, Indianapolis, IN, June 2003.

You've Got Mail. Dir. Nora Ephron. Perf. Tom Hanks, Meg Ryan. 1998. DVD. Warner Brothers, 2001.

Zimmerman, Nancy. "Research-Based Evidence: The Role of the Library Media Specialist in Reading Comprehension Instruction." *School Library Media Activities Monthly* 21 (9): 47–50 (2005).

2

SSR with Interventions Pilot Project

If we conceive of reading as a way to expand one's understanding of the world via increasing one's own understanding and literacy, then sustained silent reading is one of the greatest tools we have for building literacy.

—Elizabeth Sweeney, Classroom Teacher

ACTION RESEARCH: OUR STORY

In January 2005, we piloted an "SSR with Interventions" project. That journey of inquiry began with one question: What could we do that would be a valuable use of instruction time, make an impact on reading comprehension, engage our students, and gain buy-in from our administration? We needed our own data to prove that SSR would be valuable to students' reading achievement and to the instructional day. When discussing SSR, educators of adolescents often express concerns about how to deal with typical middle school student issues during free reading time, which include lack of interest, sleeping, and mock reading. We needed to develop a system that would gain commitment by students and staff and would meet the needs of our demographics (Figure 2.1). Thus, four classroom teachers, the library media specialist, and the district reading coordinator came together to test a model and to collect data for one possible solution. We worked to develop a program that would be simple and inexpensive to implement, as well as easy for all educators to follow. We wanted to develop action plan objectives that would improve student reading comprehension, which we thought could be met by providing time to read and reflect, and the development of stronger teacher-student relationships and more teacher involvement. If what we did

Figure 2.1.   Action Research Year Demographics

As the 12th-largest school district in Indiana, the district serves almost 14,000 students in grades K–12. The school district draws most students from the southern side of the Indianapolis metropolitan area. It has 11 elementary schools, 2 sixth-grade buildings, 2 middle schools, 2 high schools, an Alternative Education Program (by school referral only), a special services facility (special education cooperative). The district has also seen a 67.4% increase in minority population in the last six years; along with the rest of the city, a recent upsurge in the Hispanic population has changed the demographic profile of the schools.

During the action research school year, there were 52 certified classroom teachers at our school. The school's official seventh-and eighth-grade enrollment neared 1,200 students. The school had a 95% attendance rate, and 39.5% participated in the free or reduced school lunch program.

In order to begin action research, it was necessary to understand the demographics.

could have a positive impact on Indiana's state proficiency exam, ISTEP+, we would have immediate buy-in by the administration.

Forming a Plan

Today, being an educator is challenging. Educators attend trainings, staff meetings, workshops, and conferences. Educators read professional Web sites, books, journals, blogs, and subscribe to educator e-newsletters and e-mail lists. Many obsess over the quality of their instruction. And like me and most of the educators I work with, they live, breathe, and dream their jobs. It never seems enough. After all this absorption and self-doubt we continually ask ourselves, "But is it working?"

Student Achievement Analysis and Action Plan

This is a question that was posed to the educators in my building at a staff meeting. In January 2005 our principal presented to the staff a professional development growth opportunity. His goal was to get each teacher in the building to develop what he called a "Student Achievement Analysis and Action Plan." Through this prospect, each teacher would develop her own action research plan, collecting data from February through April and report findings, whether positive or negative, in May. This prospect was an ideal opportunity for professional growth. It was a unique opportunity that I had never before experienced. The principal wanted us to really think about what we were doing, why we were doing it, and whether it was effective. He was giving us the chance to test out the effectiveness of an instructional plan, but at the same time, giving us permission to make mistakes. Similar to what we ask of the students, he wanted us to go through a learning experience, an inquiry. This meant that we could try and fail or try and succeed, but either way we would learn from the experience and mature professionally. We would recognize whether what we were doing was an effective instructional practice or whether we were going down the wrong path and should stop what we were doing immediately to try another route. As our principal, Dennis Howland, stated, "While student success with your action plan is hoped for, it is not 'required.' As indicated when this professional development activity was introduced … no one will be judged or evaluated based upon the results (i.e., the success or failure) of their action plan. The process is as important as the outcome in this activity."

The Problem

It was at this same time that the National Reading Panel's Report "Teaching Children to Read" (2000), and its "Fluency" chapter (3) was being used as a reason that sustained silent reading (SSR) programs were ineffective. The report stated that "Despite widespread acceptance of the idea that schools can successfully encourage students to read more and that these increases in reading practice will be translated into better fluency and higher reading achievement, there is not adequate evidence to sustain the claim" (2000, p. 3–28). Although Stephen Krashen (2005) argued against the report, the report did establish doubt. According to Krashen, "NRP did not include long-term studies, which I found to be more supportive of sustained silent reading (SSR) than short-term studies…. Contrary to the panel's findings, I conclude that the evidence in support of free reading in school was strong" (p. 444). But the damage had already been done. Teachers, administrators, and schools incorporating free voluntary reading into the instructional day were questioning its value. We were no exception. We had been trying to build SSR into the instructional day for years, and the report and its ramifications became a serious roadblock. But now we could use the Student Achievement Analysis and our Action Plan as our vehicle for proving SSR's merit with our own students.

During the staff meeting that introduced the principal's professional development program, I knew this was our opportunity. He was giving us the chance to try something new, implement a program, and learn from the experience. This was our opportunity to take conflicting reports from experts and use them as a springboard for our own action research. Immediately after the staff meeting, I was approached by a few classroom teachers. They wanted to know what my thoughts were and as we talked, I realized this could be the break I had been looking for with SSR.

Formulating a Plan

After talking with some classroom teachers, I met with the principal. Principals feel a great deal of pressure to improve standardized test scores. A measure of this pressure was reflected in our principal asking his staff to look at the classroom and analyze the effectiveness of what we were doing. He wanted to increase the level of student active engagement in the classroom. One of his concerns with traditional SSR was that not enough students were "actively engaged." Once the concept was presented to him, with intervention strategies outlined, he was skeptical but willing to give us the opportunity to try it. I summarized for him a very basic outline of the SSR with Interventions concept and the possibility of pulling together a small group of teachers to pilot the project for our action research project. I outlined to the principal what I wanted to do, discussed the need to implement the action plan as a group, and the need to include the district reading coordinator in the plan. The meeting went very well and, with a few additional requirements of his own, the concept was approved.

Initially, the action research group began with the library media specialist and one seventh-grade Language Arts teacher. Alison Hart was in agreement from the initial discussions and stated, "I was looking for a way to enhance the SSR process to hold kids more accountable for what they read. When I addressed my concern with [the library media specialist], she approached me with the idea of guided SSR in the classroom. The idea really appealed to me because in my classroom, one-on-one interaction is a necessity for my students to learn. At the time that [the library media specialist] and I began the process, our building principal assigned the staff with an Action Research project. We were able to choose our research as long as we could prove we were 'owning our own data' and trying to improve our school goals in the School Improvement Plan (which would include ISTEP+). This went hand-in-hand with my goal of increasing student accountability and tracking their progress."

Because of my limited experience with action research, we wanted to keep the group small—no more than four teachers' classes. Once word spread, interest grew. Soon a seventh-grade Language Arts teacher volunteered, and shortly thereafter, I approached an eighth-grade Focus (basic skills course) teacher who agreed to joined the venture. Once discussions began with our school district reading coordinator, a content area teacher was invited (Geometry/Algebra) and agreed to participate. This addition of a math teacher was helpful because she was a content area teacher with no reading training, and her class consisted of advanced and gifted and talented students, a group not yet represented in the study. Nancy Meyer-Brown, the reading coordinator, felt that it was important to invite an educator to pilot the program who was not related to Language Arts, so that we would have a perspective of how easy it would be to implement in any classroom, and if it was successful, we would more easily gain buy-in from teachers of other disciplines.

With the support of the school district's reading coordinator, classroom teachers, and library media specialist, the outline of the program and what we hoped to achieve was developed. Classroom teachers voiced concerns about students who were sleeping, mock reading, or distracting others during classroom SSR. What could we do that would be a valuable use of instruction time, engage our students, and gain loyalty from our administration? With those concerns in mind, we worked to develop a program that would be simple to implement and easy for teachers to follow.

The Solution

Once we had all the key players in place and our ideas outlined, I began drafting the action plan. The action plan, as outlined by our school principal, included a goal, written in the form of a learning objective, materials needed, formative assessment, and activities to meet objectives. Our foundational goal, which never changed, was to increase student's reading comprehension scores. We agreed that we would be piloting a project of guided SSR, which would include educator-intervention strategies.

Working collaboratively through the application, we met as a group and e-mailed edits and revisions back and forth until all were in agreement and satisfied. Once the plan was approved by the group, we turned in a final copy to the principal. We agreed the objective would be met through:

- Stronger monitoring of students to ensure all students are reading;
- Engaging in one-on-one student-teacher conversations related to student's reading;
- 10–20 minute SSR three to five times per week;

- Concluding SSR with a reading-writing prompt and student's journaling in a "reading-writing-response" journal;
- Maintaining a teacher SSR journal.

Getting Ready

We needed to get started right away. We were under a tight timeline as outlined by our principal, but we also had to contend with the issue that, if we started right away, we had only three months to incorporate SSR with Interventions before we had to wrap things up. Such a small amount of time might be a problem because, as Krashen (2004, 2005) concluded, long-term studies are more supportive of SSR. We were confined to a finite amount of time:

September 2004	ISTEP+
October 2004	NWEA test
January 2005	Pre-Attitudinal Survey, SSR with Interventions classroom activities begin
April 2005	NWEA test, Post-Attitudinal Survey, SSR with Interventions ends
September 2005	ISTEP+

It was important that this project be inexpensive, but we knew we had some basic supply needs. Because we had almost everything we needed, the only expense to implementing our SSR with Interventions action research was a resource binder of instructional resources for participating classroom teachers and a stenographer notepad for each student. The reading coordinator put together a resource binder for each of the classroom teachers. We also needed to have something for students to use for journals, so I negotiated a discounted price for steno pads for each student to use. With the principal's support, I wrote a grant to the Parent-Teacher Association (PTA) requesting financial support for this expense. Any time we ran into a snag, our principal was our problem solver. When our grant request went to the PTA, he spoke in support of the project and grant.

Access to a variety of books was important. The library media center schedule included 20 minutes each week for every class to visit for self-selected reading. Students could use this time to browse the library media center collection and select books related to their interests and abilities. Classroom bookshelves had already been established. Every classroom had a small classroom bookshelf stocked with paperbacks for the adolescent reader, and the library media center maintained a healthy stock of paperbacks for trading and refilling classroom bookshelves.

We needed to inform parents of the action research, so I composed a letter to send home to parents. Before it was sent home, the letter was peer-edited by the participating classroom teachers, then approved by the principal. Classroom teachers explained to students the importance of the letter and the importance of taking it home and showing it to parents. Students were told, and a letter sent to the parents explained, that even if families did not give permission to include a child's data in the action research process, the student would still be responsible for all work and instructional activities. It was written as a letter of consent (Figure 2.2), which meant that it informed parents of the program, the need to collect the data, and the parent did not need to return the

Figure 2.2. Action Research Assumption of Consent Parent Letter

January 10, 2005

Dear Parent/Guardian:

Your child's class has been selected to participate in a data collection project. The goal is to evaluate the value of silent sustained reading (SSR) to students' reading abilities and attitudes.

How will we do this? During this semester, selected classes will take a pre- and post computerized NWEA (Northwest Evaluation Association) reading growth and comprehension tests as well as pre- and post attitudinal reading surveys. Throughout the semester all participating classes, as part of SSR, will have regular and frequent times for silent reading and journaling in a 'reading-writing-response log.'

It is assumed that all students in the participating classes will participate in the data collection project, however, if you **do not** wish your child to contribute to this opportunity for educators to better understand the student learning process, please date, print your name, sign your name, print your child's name, and return this letter before January 14, 2005. Letters not returned will be an assumption of student participation.

Students not supplying data for the data collection project will still be required to participate and complete all SSR activities. If you have any questions or concerns, please contact Mrs. Preddy by phone,*<school phone number here>*, or email *<email address here>*.

Leslie B. Preddy
School Library Media Specialist

An informational letter of consent on school letterhead was sent home to parents prior to beginning the classroom activities.

letter unless the parent would not allow us to include his child's data in the analysis. Signing and returning the letter meant that we would not include the child's data, but the student would still be responsible for participating in all classroom activities.

Teachers designated a location in the classroom to store the student reading-writing-response journals, which were spiral-bound steno pads. Most kept them in a corner of the room in a storage crate reserved for this purpose. The journals were only taken out during SSR with Interventions and remained in the classroom at all times.

By mid-January everything was organized and ready, and classroom teachers introduced the program to students. Student participation began with a pre-attitudinal survey. Student attitudes were important to improving reading comprehension. Kay Bishop, in *Connecting Libraries with Classrooms,* states: "The reason for low student test scores

TABLE 2.1
Pre-Attitudinal Survey—Question Average Score: January 2005

	Results Average 1 = Agree, 0 = Disagree									
Question	1	2	3	4	5	6	7	8	9	10
Grade 7	0.7	0.6	0.7	0.2	0.6	0.8	0.8	0.6	0.6	0.1
Grade 8	0.8	0.4	0.6	0.3	0.8	0.8	0.9	0.8	0.7	0.0

The quantitative results of the attitudinal survey were given a numerical code, which was entered into an Excel spreadsheet for analysis. Each question response received a 0 for a negative and a 1 for an affirmative response, giving each question a maximum value of 1.

can be contributed not only to not being able to read, but also the negative attitudes toward reading itself" (2003, p. 69). Our survey was developed by the reading coordinator and Dr. James Hatfield, the school psychologist. Students responded to quantitative and qualitative questions. The 10 quantitative question responses were marked in an agree or disagree column:

Having an opportunity to read on my own in school is important to me.
Reading helps me in my daily life.
Prior to reading, I make predictions as to what the book will be about by looking at pictures, title, and cover.
During reading, I make note of personal connections in what the author says and what I think.
During reading, I can stop, pause, and think about what I just read.
During reading, if I get stuck, I know what to do.
After reading, I can tell the theme of the story.
After reading, I can adjust my predictions and draw conclusions.
I read more than 10 minutes a day.
I use a journal to jot down my thoughts when I finish reading.

When we examined each individual question, we found that survey results averaged fairly positive toward most questions. We were especially surprised at the affirmative response to "Having an opportunity to read on my own in school is important to me." This signaled to us that our students should be surprisingly open to adding reading time to their instructional day. Question 4 received one of the lowest scores, which hinted at a need for our students to take more time to think and reflect about what they are reading. Question 10's low score did not surprise us. Although middle school students spend a lot of time writing notes, instant messaging, and blogging, most don't include reading experiences in their journaling or keep a private journal.

The quantitative aspect of the pre-attitudinal survey was given the potential sum of 10. There were 10 questions and each positive response received a value of 1, a negative response a 0. Student composite pre-attitudinal survey scores were mid-range and disappointing, with grade seven scoring lower than eighth grade. Surprisingly to us, though, was the eighth-grade class composed of advanced and gifted and talented students that ranked what we felt was a low attitudinal score (6.58) for students with above average reading competencies. The average student score, of all classes and students combined, was 5.66.

TABLE 2.2
Pre-Attitudinal Survey—Average Cumulative Score: January 2005

	Results Average 10-point Range				
Grade 7	Group A	5.21	Grade 8	Group C	5.15
	Group B	5.80		G/T-Advanced	6.58
	Average	5.48		Average	6.10
				Combined average	**5.66**

The maximum potential sum, cumulative score, of each student's attitudinal survey was 10 points. All groups combined pre-attitudinal score average was 5.66.

The four qualitative questions were open-ended for personal reflection and response. Pre-attitudinal survey quantitative responses were varied, but most seemed to focus on the negative feeling and opinions about reading. Below is a sampling of common responses, including the student's original grammar, spelling, and punctuation.

What words pop into your mind when you think of reading a book?

boring
nothing cause I be to busy reading.
I think, "Man, that [stinks]."
It depends on what kind of mood I'm in …
none
It depends on what book it is. If it's a school book its like here we go again.

How do you find books you love to read?

look at the title and cover
I go to the library.
I read the back of the book.
Just go to the computer, put in the title of the book, and I can find online

The things I am great at as a reader are …

short books
none
I can commprihend things easily
I can read a book when I want to.
I sometimes have problems with words.

Things I need to work on to improve my reading are …

try to remember the words I read.
read more
Speed, cause I SLow!
Improve how I read.
read lyrics
nothing!
flow
…learn to like reading

Figure 2.3. District and Building Level Goals

2003–2008 District Strategic Plan

Goal 2: Focus on What and How Each Student Learns
  Objective 4: Ensure that all students are effective readers.
  Objective 5: Create relevance in schools in order to motivate each student.

School NCA/PL221 School Improvement Goal

Increase student performance with the Indiana Academic Standard, *Reading Comprehension.*

School district and building goals were fundamental to our action research plan.

Implementing SSR with Interventions

Once the surveys were complete, educators implemented the instructional aspects of SSR with Interventions. It was important to make the most effective use of instructional time, so as we developed our instructional plan, we needed to address our Indiana Academic Standards, school and district goals, ISTEP+, access to books, and the emotional needs of our students. With those guiding principles, we arrived at the following basic needs to be met:

Reading for enjoyment
Managing informational text
Reflecting upon reading through writing/journaling
Experiencing educator involvement.

Candy Schaefer, Language Arts teacher, found many benefits after implementing our plan: "When I began the guided SSR, our SSR time seemed to come together, it was more structured and the students knew what to expect. Monday through Wednesday it was student choice, Thursday was Newspaper Activity, and Friday was *Scope* or *Action* magazine day. Students would get excited about things they had read and want to share with me or the class. Students also discovered genres, and which one or ones they preferred. Students were also able to make personal connections to fiction and nonfiction works."

Sustained Silent Reading

During the action research time, classes were asked to establish a routine and engage in SSR with Interventions three to five times a week. All classroom teachers chose to participate every day, with the occasional day off because of other instructional conflicts (tests, field trips, etc.).

Free choice reading was offered three to four days a week. On these days, students could read from any format they chose: novel, graphic novel, comic book, short story, etc. The only restriction was no textbook or school assignment reading.

Informational text reading was selected one to two days each week. I would glance through magazines and newspapers as they arrived in the library media center or at home, looking for material for informational text days. Articles of interest were shared with classroom teachers, but the final choice of the material was up to the classroom teacher. Elizabeth Sweeney, Focus teacher, found that "due to the variety of texts we studied (newspapers, non-fiction magazines, catalogues, novels), students became more comfortable negotiating diverse texts. For example, at the beginning of the project, many students had never read a newspaper in their lives except for occasionally checking sports statistics. After the SSR project, every student can now locate various types of information in a major newspaper, identify the sections, and state the relevance of knowledge found in a newspaper."

Classroom teachers were encouraged to read aloud and booktalk to students. They were persuaded to use anything they had made a personal connection or material they felt were powerful or thought students would make a personal connection: a passage from a novel, poetry, short story, essay, editorial, article, comic, letter, quote, etc.

Reading-Writing-Response Journal

We needed a writing prompt for every free choice reading day. The prompts needed to be generic, or applicable to what every student in the room might be reading. We did not know where to begin finding generic writing prompts for use with the students so we worked together to come up with our own. Participating classroom teachers were asked to e-mail me approximately five generic prompts she had created. Once compiled, I distributed the list to the group. This gave us enough prompts to get the program started.

During SSR, the prompt was displayed in a prominent location before reading began, giving the students a chance to ponder it before they began reading. At the conclusion of silent reading time, students would get out their reading-writing-response journal, enter details about what they read, and then spend the next three to five minutes relating to their reading by writing a response to the prompt.

Classroom teachers also kept a daily log, or journal, keeping track of what they read, the writing prompt used for the day, and notes about conferences, or interviews, held with students.

Access to Books

Student were encouraged to bring reading material to school and class. Each classroom also had a classroom bookshelf from which students could pick reading material. There was a special collection, not processed or cataloged, in a library media center workroom of books classroom teachers could take to replenish their classroom bookshelves as books began to disappear. Classroom teachers were encouraged not to be concerned about books disappearing from their classroom bookshelves and finding new homes. Classes were scheduled to come to the library media center weekly for self-selected reading, book check-out time. In the library media center, students could browse the shelves and search by specific interest on the OPAC (online public access catalog). The library media specialist and classroom teacher worked together to give informal, persuasive booktalks and assist students in locating a book to meet the student's personal interests and needs.

Emotional Needs = Teacher Involvement

Meeting the emotional needs of students meant that educators needed to have a committed reading presence. Students needed classroom teachers who were reading, and visible. Educator involvement included reading, reading promotion, student conferencing, and responding to student journals.

Reading promotion had three basic components: modeling reading, booktalks, and reading aloud. Every day classroom teachers were expected to begin SSR by reading, just as the students read. The classroom teachers also had free choice and selected adolescent literature, professional materials, and adult literature as their SSR reading material.

Classroom teachers were encouraged to share their reading expertise and interests. They could do that by booktalking reads that they thought students might enjoy reading themselves and reading aloud pieces that they found moving, enjoyable, or great for reading aloud. Students at first grumbled at being treated like babies by being read to, but Alison Hart was surprised to find that soon, "They would beg me to read to them."

Student conferencing was vitally important. Once SSR had settled in for the day, the teacher would set her reading aside and hold conversations about books, reading interests, or reading comprehension individually with students. She would interview as many students each day as necessary to make sure each student had his personal time with the classroom teacher each week. Candy Schaefer commented, "SSR [with Interventions] helped because by finding out what genres each student is more interested in, it helped me to make a personal connection with each student, especially when going to the [library media center]. When I got a new book for the classroom bookshelf I would let the whole class know. I would also speak directly to the students I knew might have a keen interest in that book. It is almost like building a different kind of trust with the students."

Just as teachers interacted with students through personal conversations, they also responded to students' reading-writing-response journals. This was the only portion of instruction that needed to be done outside of SSR time. Every week the classroom teacher wrote at least one personal comment, response, or suggestion in each student's journal. So that reading the journal would not be a time-management burden, the journals were kept in the classroom and it was expected that each journal needed to be reviewed only once a week, therefore, only a few needed to be read each day. Elizabeth Sweeney stated: "It was easy to respond to the journals a bit at a time that way. Whenever I had even five or ten minutes, I could respond to the students' writing. I did not have to rely on middle-schoolers to bring their journals in for me to assess, nor did I have to read every journal at the same time. Having the steno pads close at hand simplified assessment and allowed constant monitoring of student progress and engagement."

The Results

Now was the time to see if we had made any difference for our students. With a three-month timeline, we grew nervous wondering whether we had implemented the project long enough to see results. To gauge whether students' reading comprehension actually improved, I worked with Dr. James Hatfield, school district psychologist, to interpret the data. Honestly, I was more than slightly intimidated by statistics and did not want to misinterpret the results. Dr. Hatfield's willingness to join the collaborative team and work with us to analyze the data was invaluable. We collected data through a variety of means and for different purposes.

- ISTEP+ (Indiana Statewide Testing for Education Progress) fall 2004 (pre-) and fall 2005 (post-) English/Language Arts (E/LA) to gauge any improvement on the annual state proficiency exam.

TABLE 2.3
School and Sample Group Population: 2004–2005 School Year

	Student population	Participating students	Students included in data analysis
Grade 7	627	151	121
Grade 8	558	87	40
Total	1,186	238	161

We began the project with 238 students, 20% of the school's student population.

- NWEA fall 2004 to spring 2005 "Lang Survey IN Version 2" tests to evaluate reading comprehension growth.
- Pre- to Post-Attitudinal Surveys to analyze any effect the program might have on student reading attitudes.
- Classroom Teacher's SSR Journal for an overview of classroom climate and student engagement.
- Classroom Teacher's Post-Project Survey to gain an educator's professional perspective on the program and classroom climate.

We concluded the project with 161 students, 14 percent of the school population, with viable data. Those 161 students came from four teachers, two seventh-grade and two eighth-grade. Twenty-five students were labeled G/T (Gifted/Talented) or Advanced. Three students were in the ENL (English as a New Language) program. Fourteen students had IEP's (Individual Education Plans) for a learning or emotional disability.

As usually happens when collecting data in a school, we began the project with a larger number of students than ended up in our final results. We lost just a handful from parents returning the assumption of consent letter and requesting a child's data be excluded. From one eighth-grade teacher, we lost 50 students from the data analysis because of missing fall NWEA or ISTEP+ tests score, so we had no initial data to compare. In some cases the student's fall test results were available, but the student withdrew before we could conduct the spring NWEA test in April.

We found it difficult to analyze the eighth-grade data because of the G/T and Advanced students in that group. According to Krashen (2005), "In-school reading programs are likely to be of greatest benefit to less mature readers, for they provide reading exposure and get students interested in reading" (p. 446). The advanced and G/T students already read regularly and had fine reading comprehension scores. It would follow that a student with a high score to begin with would not have as much growth, because there was not much room for improvement.

As the library media specialist and project coordinator, I entered each student's name, grade, teacher, course, NWEA, ISTEP+ and quantitative attitudinal survey results into an Excel spreadsheet. Dr. Hatfield then analyzed the data. He was instrumental in explaining to us what all of our numbers meant to the project.

ISTEP+ and State English/Language Arts Proficiency

We had to wait a year to evaluate the impact on the test that matters most to administrators: the state proficiency exam. Through these results, we would learn whether our students

TABLE 2.4
Grade 7 ISTEP+ English/Language Arts Scores

	Fall 2004 (Grade 7)			Fall 2005 (Grade 8)			ISTEP+ Pass	
	Number of students	Score average	Minimum pass score	Number of students	Score average	Minimum pass score	Expected growth	Actual growth
Students not in group	476	508	497	503	528	516	+19	**+20**
Students in SSR group	103	489	497	103	516	516	+19	+27

The average ISTEP+ score for participating seventh-grade students improved from DNP (Did Not Pass) prior to participation to a passing score the year following SSR with Interventions.

met the state's minimum growth expected for the grade level and whether they fared better or worse than those students not participating in the action research project. Although the rest of the action research results were based on three-month student participation, ISTEP+ results were based on four months. This is because participating classroom teachers considered the program too important to stop. Although the action research concluded in April with the post–NWEA test and attitudinal survey, all participating classroom teachers opted to continue SSR with Interventions through to the end of the school year in May.

It was reported in a December 2005 press release that statewide ISTEP+ "results showed student scores improving or remaining level at all grades tested in 2005" (Indiana Department of Education). Our school fell into the "scores improving" category, but our students were still under the state average. Examining the average score of all the school's seventh and eighth graders, we could see that scores were improving from year to year, but even with improvement, the school was still slightly below the state average.

The seventh-grade fall 2004 ISTEP+ E/LA minimum score for passing was 497; participating students score average was 489, eight points below passing. These students are what we call "bubble" kids. Our school had been focusing on getting these just-below-passing bubble kids into the passing range. The seventh-grade students who participated in our action research now had a fall 2005 ISTEP+ E/LA average score of 516. The eighth-grade minimum score for passing was 516. The expected growth from seventh-grade to eighth-grade year was 19 points. Our participating students' average growth was 27 points. Our participating students had not only gained more than expected, but the student average moved from DNP (Did Not Pass) to passing.

We ran into a slight roadblock with the eighth-grade group's data. Because of being unable to use the data for most of the participating eighth graders in our "regular" group, we did not have enough students with usable data. Although we had 57 regular eighth-grade students participate in the project, only 14 had both scores necessary for comparing pre- and post- results for the tests (NWEA, ISTEP+, attitudinal survey). Because of the small sample, we only looked at the eighth-grade G/T-Advanced students' ISTEP+ scores. Twenty-two of the participating G/T-Advanced students had usable I-STEP data, enough students to be a viable group to analyze.

TABLE 2.5
Grade 8 G/T and Advanced ISTEP+ English/Language Arts Scores

G/T – Advanced	Fall 2004 (Grade 8)				Fall 2005 (Grade 9)				ISTEP+	
	Number of students	Score average	Minimum pass score	Minimum pass+ score	Number of students	Score average	Minimum pass score	Minimum pass+ score	Expected growth (pass/ pass+)	Actual growth
Students not in group	114	575	516	611	114	601	521	643	+5 / +32	**+26**
Students in SSR group	22	594	516	611	22	633	521	643	+5 / +32	**+39**

The average ISTEP+ score for participating eighth-grade G/T-Advanced students was greater than expected growth.

ISTEP+ scores are arranged into three major categories: Did Not Pass (DNP), Pass, Pass+. Students in G/T and Advanced classes are expected to be in the Pass+ range. Students' scores are expected to improve from eighth- to ninth-grade year by 5 points for Pass, with a 32-point improvement for Pass+ students. G/T-Advanced average score improved by +39, greater growth than expected and 13 points more growth than the G/T-Advanced students not in the project group, a significant difference.

NWEA and Reading Comprehension

Student reading comprehension growth was measured with the NWEA fall 2004 and spring 2005 "Lang Survey IN Version 2" test. After I entered the results into the Excel spreadsheet, Dr. Hatfield analyzed the NWEA scores and based his results on RIT scores. According to Dr. Hatfield: "RIT scores (Rasch Unit) are used to describe student achievement and growth on the NWEA Measures of Academic Progress. They are on an equal interval, longitudinal scale, so they are well suited to observing achievement growth over time, across grade levels. They are referenced to the curriculum in the areas of Reading, Language Use, Math and Science, if administered. Scores can range from about 150 to 300."

The average RIT growth for both grades combined (excluding the G/T and Advanced students) was +7.70, expected RIT growth is 3.5. This is a statistically significant difference. Seventy-five percent of our students (excluding G/T and Advanced) had greater annual RIT growth than is expected. Participating seventh-grade teacher Alison Posey remarked, "[Students] who normally don't have time to read full stories or books had time and their scores definitely went up. I was very pleased and excited for them."

For seventh grade, fall to spring average RIT growth was +8.01. Expected RIT growth is 3.5. Dr. Hatfield found a "statistically significant difference, greater growth than is expected from fall to spring with seventh grade participating students' NWEA scores."

There was an inconsistency with the eighth-grade participating students' NWEA scores where growth was less than expected from NWEA norms. For eighth grade, fall to spring average RIT growth was 2.63. Expected RIT growth is 3.4. This was not a statistically significant change. Interpreting these scores could have been complicated by the

TABLE 2.6
NWEA English/Language Arts Average Scores and RIT Growth

	Number of students	Fall 2004 scores	Spring 2005 scores	RIT growth	Expected growth
Grade 7	121	208.64	216.64	**8.01**	3.5
Grade 8	40	228.18	230.80	2.63	3.4
G-T/Advanced	26	233.69	235.00	1.31	3.4
Regular	14	217.93	223.00	**5.07**	3.4

Participating students' NWEA scores showed greater growth than expected from fall to spring. Participants in seventh grade had a statistically significant change.

inclusion of G/T-Advanced participant scores. The remaining eighth graders, removing the eighth-grade G/T and Advanced, showed a growth of +5.07, greater than expected.

Post-Attitudinal Survey

Student attitudinal survey quantitative data was analyzed using Microsoft Excel by giving a numerical score to the checked agree or disagree survey. The score range was 0–10, with 10 being the highest positive score. Averaging scores, all groups' average post-attitudinal survey responses increased toward the positive. The eighth grade averaged a slightly greater gain. According to the attitudinal survey, the average total score of *all* groups' attitudes toward reading and reading for pleasure improved by +0.83 on the 10-point scale.

Surprising us, the G/T-Advanced had an attitudinal gain, +0.54. We were intrigued by the fact that the kids with the best reading comprehension and ISTEP+ scores had surprisingly low attitudinal score in the beginning and a positive attitudinal gain. The G/T-Advanced students considered reading an educational responsibility. Although these students didn't need the "practice" reading that SSR provides, they needed SSR with Interventions, and our help locating the joy and comfort found in reading for pleasure's sake.

TABLE 2.7
Attitudinal Survey: Pre- and Post-Cumulative Scores, January 2005–April 2005

	Results Average Cumulated Score (10-point Range)		
	Pre-	Post-	Difference
Grade 7	5.48	6.31	+0.83
Group A	5.21	6.44	+1.23
Group B	5.80	6.16	+0.36
Grade 8	6.10	6.95	+0.85
Group C	5.15	6.62	+1.47
G/T-Advanced	6.58	7.12	+0.54
All students	5.66	6.49	+0.83

With a maximum possible score of 10, all groups had positive overall growth according to the attitudinal survey.

TABLE 2.8
Grade 7 Attitudinal Survey—Question Results

	Results Average 1 = Agree, 0 = Disagree									
Question	1	2	3	4	5	6	7	8	9	10
Pre-	0.66	0.62	0.73	0.20	0.64	0.76	0.77	0.59	0.62	0.07
Post-	0.63	0.77	0.76	0.40	0.72	0.83	0.77	0.67	0.72	0.24
Difference	−0.03	+0.15	+0.03	**+0.20**	+0.12	+0.07	–	+0.08	+0.10	+0.17

Students in the seventh-grade group had a significant positive change to question 4.

Analyzing each individual question, we found that most survey questions' pre- and post- scores remained the same or increased among all groups. Survey question 4, "During reading, I make note of personal connections in what the author says and what I think" received a significant positive gain in the seventh grade and eighth-grade regular group. This related to our efforts to communicate with the students during reading conferences and the students reflecting on their reading by journaling.

The greatest gains, and statistically significant difference, for all groups were the eighth-grade regular students +0.28 gain for question 4, "During reading, I make note of personal connections in what the author says and what I think." It is also important to note their significant +0.21 gain with question 9, "I read more than 10 minutes a day." Grade seven also had a positive change of +0.20 with question 4 and +0.15 with question 2, "Reading helps me in my daily life." As classroom teacher Candy Schaefer, explained, "I believe most students' reading behavior changed as they became more fluent and began to comprehend what they had read. The students have to read everyday and knowing that they are accountable for a journal concerning their reading, was influential toward their reading. They could

TABLE 2.9
Grade 8 Attitudinal Survey—Question Results

	Results Average 1 = Agree, 0 = Disagree									
Question	1	2	3	4	5	6	7	8	9	10
8th-Grade Gifted/Talented and Advanced										
Pre-	0.88	0.42	0.62	0.42	0.81	0.77	0.92	0.85	0.88	0.00
Post-	0.92	0.46	0.65	0.42	0.73	0.88	0.96	0.88	0.96	0.23
Difference	+0.04	+0.04	+0.03	–	-0.08	+0.11	+0.04	+0.03	+0.08	**+0.23**
8th-Grade Regular										
Pre-	0.79	0.40	0.63	0.20	0.80	0.79	0.87	0.71	0.63	0.04
Post-	0.83	0.57	0.72	0.48	0.72	0.88	0.88	0.76	0.84	0.28
Difference	+0.04	+0.17	+0.09	**+0.28**	-0.08	+0.09	+0.01	+0.05	**+0.21**	+0.24

The eighth-grade G/T-Advanced group had a significant positive change to question 10 and the eighth-grade regular had a significant positive change to questions 4, 9 and 10.

not 'fake' the writing prompt or my questions concerning the reading. So in turn, practice makes perfect or in this case improves greatly." These gains were important to establishing lifelong reading habits. Collaborating teacher Elizabeth Sweeney emphasized: "This was one of the most significant triumphs of the project! So often at the beginning, I heard, 'I don't like to read. I'm not good at it.' Yet after having been given time and resources to read in class each day, students become much more comfortable interacting with different types of texts. They could open a newspaper to the editorial page, explain why they agreed or disagreed with a column, and respond to a letter to the editor. They could summarize the plot and theme of fiction both verbally and in writing. They could identify the main point of non-fiction texts. Additionally, students were increasingly able to make personal connections to various texts. If we conceive of reading as a way to expand one's understanding of the world via increasing one's own understanding and literacy, then sustained silent reading is one of the greatest tools we have for building literacy. When we do not compel students to read texts within a given time frame, much of their anxiety lessens and their confidence grows. Perhaps this is due to processing ability and speed: those experiencing emergent literacy are not forced to keep up with highly literate readers."

Students responded to the same four qualitative questions on the post-attitudinal survey as they did on the pre-attitudinal survey. Post-project responses were surprisingly improved. Student responses became more positive, thoughtful, and they took more ownership than with the pre-attitudinal surveys. Below is a sample of post-project responses, including the student's original grammar, spelling, and punctuation.

What words pop into your mind when you think of reading a book?

- Excitement
- …Something you can connect to.
- "I hope it's a good one"
- I'm tired, this is not a good book.—This is a good book, I'm hungrey.
- adventure, romance, funny, scary, and, exciting

How do you find books you love to read?

- Check online
- the back of the book
- Go in the computer and write a title of a book…
- …school books (from library).
- I look at the cover and read the back, then I read the first page.
- I go to the library.
- Teachers …

The things I am great at as a reader are …

- sounding out words
- Imagining the story in my mind
- I can consintrate
- Not stopping …
- I can see pictures in my head

Things I need to work on to improve my reading are …

- work on reading comprehension
- read more per day

Figure 2.4. Attitudinal Survey Qualitative Question Sample Comparison

Qualitative question	Pre-project response	Post-project response
What words pop into your mind when you think of reading a book?	"boring, [dumb], stupid, waste of time, time to take a nap."	"Love, action, sad, mystery"
How do you find books you love to read?	"I don't because I don't like to read at all"	"By the cover and the back"
The things I am great at as a reader are . . .	"Nothing because I don't read"	"Getting done with a book if I enjoy it."
Things I need to work on to improve my reading are . . .	"Reading more than I usually do. Stay awake while I am reading."	"Pick better books that interest me and I enjoy."

Sample of the opinion changes in reader maturity that occurred in a student after three months of SSR with Interventions. Student's original grammar, spelling, and punctuation have been retained.

- Reading more.
- Read more and try to remember what I read ...
- learn more complicated words
- use my imagination more and try to see what I am reading in my head

Classroom Teacher's Journal and Professional Observations

Classroom teachers maintained a log, or journal, along with students. As students journaled a response to their reading based on the writing prompt provided by the teacher, the teacher wrote in her journal. Classroom teachers were asked to maintain daily notes about the date, time given to SSR, writing prompt selected, notes about students who were conferenced that day, personal observations, impressions about students' reading-writing-response journals, and of great importance to the SSR with Interventions data, the number or percentage of students on/off task during SSR. Classroom teachers reported students' pretend reading or sleeping dissipated and active participation and engagement in SSR increased to 100 percent by the end of February, just weeks after implementation.

Classroom teachers felt students' reading-writing-response journals progressed well. Teachers reported that as the project progressed there was an increased quantity of words in the student reflection, increased vocabulary, and increased "connectivity."

Classroom teachers reported students' active participation in SSR increased to 100 percent by the end of February, just weeks after implementing the program. According to one teacher's post- survey response, "I noticed students who, at the beginning who said they didn't like to read, became more engaged with whatever they were reading and began to ask questions that related to the text. Some of the students also recognized their own improvement."

Classroom Teacher's Post-Project Survey

I developed a classroom teacher post-project survey, which was reviewed and approved by the reading coordinator, and completed by each of the four classroom teachers participating in the pilot project.

- What sort of conversations did you hold with students related to self-selected readings prior to this project?
- Did those conversations (content, quality, personal connections, etc) change throughout this project? If yes, please explain.
- Did the guided SSR project impact or influence your relationship with students? Explain why or why not.
- What sort of impact, if any, did this guided SSR project have on your daily classroom management and instruction?
- What changes, if any, occurred on your observation checklist as the guided SSR project progressed?
- Describe the behavior of the students at the inception of incorporating SSR in the classroom.
- Describe the behavior of the students at the conclusion of the year of SSR in the classroom.
- Explain how students' reading behavior changed or did not change (and your educated guess as to why).
- Explain how students' confidence in reading ability changed or did not change (and your educated guess as to why).
- Additional comments.

Responses were thoughtful, considerate, and filled with constructive criticism, including suggestions for improvements. Among the comment made by classroom teachers on the post-project survey were:

- "The guided SSR helped in classroom management, because it was the first activity of the day. The students knew to come into the class, get a book, magazine, or newspaper, and sit in their assigned seat before the bell would ring."
- " … students adjusted and knew this was a relaxing time."
- "There was structure and routine. Students would get on each other when they didn't have books … "
- "At the beginning of SSR the students seemed to drag their feet, however as time passed I noticed how they seemed to enjoy it more."
- "I got so used to the silence that I became less tolerant of noise in my other classes. I do not think it affected my instruction too much except it did raise my expectations in terms of the ability of middle-schoolers to engage in sustained silent reading and behave maturely."
- "Throughout the project, we discussed what students like to read: mostly magazines, especially those related to video games and celebrities. Students were able to respond to oral and written questions about plot, character, relevance of texts to own lives, theme, and quality of writing. As I spent more time with each student, our conversations often strayed into plans for the future, school success, likes and dislikes, etc."

- "It did change for the better. Many were not afraid to read in front of others and also they commented on how much faster they could finish stories and correctly answer questions."
- "One day I decided not to have SSR, to give them a break, I was pleasantly surprised how many students were upset at missing their reading time; so, we had SSR. Many students, who would not normally finish a book, finished at least two books. Some students began to read 'novel series,' it was very exciting to see how enthusiastic they became about reading."

What Went Wrong
(or If We Knew Then What We Know Now)

An important aspect of action research is to learn as you progress through the experience. Learn from mistakes as well as successes. As our depth of understanding grew and our knowledge of the process improved, we had "aha" moments provided by hindsight.

Pre- and Post-Attitudinal Survey

The problems we had with the attitudinal survey were that not all students answered every pre- and post- survey question; students sometimes chose to mark the dividing line between agree and disagree (those marks were given a 0.5 score); and some students had difficulty understanding the language of the survey questions as well as the terms *agree* and *disagree*. We should have developed a definition and clear instructions for the students prior to having them complete the surveys. As a result of our errors, students left some questions blank. By default we had to give a blank (no score) in the spreadsheet, which equated to a 0, or negative, response. Students should have been told that all questions must be answered. Some indecisive students answered, but couldn't decide whether to fully agree or disagree, so instead placed their mark directly in the middle, which in our data analysis we gave a partial score of 0.5.

Random Sampling

Should we have thought more carefully about which classes to include? Our groups were pure random selection. Because of that completely random choosing, and our false assumption that most students would have a fall NWEA reading comprehension score, we had to remove the data from the majority of our eighth-grade regular students, which didn't leave us with enough students for an appropriate statistical sampling.

G/T-Advanced

Should we have included a class full of advanced and gifted and talented students? Including them made our eighth-grade data unusable because we realized later that we should pull the G/T-Advanced and consider them a third group, separate from the 7th and 8th grade groups. The students already had high reading comprehension scores before the action research began, so potential growth would not be so noteworthy (Krashen 2005). But they are also a group we learned from and who surprised us in the end. The beginning attitudes about reading stunned us by being so low, so excluding them from the onset may have eliminated an opportunity for us to learn something about these high-performing students. They also showed the greatest growth in their state standardized scores, which was another surprise to us. So eliminating G/T-Advanced completely would have been a mistake, but making them a third group and adding more to the eighth grade group would have resolved our numbers problem.

CONCLUSION

The SSR with Interventions project was introduced to students in mid-January and officially concluded at the end of April, but participating teachers believed in the program so much that they voluntarily continued the program through the end of the school year. As Candy Schaefer said, "I like the SSR [with Interventions] and plan on continuing it throughout my teaching career, especially after finding out the increased NWEA and ISTEP+ scores. I truly believe it works!" We were able to develop a simple and easy-to-follow program that was an effective use of instructional time. With just three months of this intervention, participating students' reading comprehension scores increased more than expected; students showed improved attitudes toward reading based on the attitudinal surveys; and after four months of participating students, state standardized E/LA test score improvement was greater than students who did not participate in the program. This was just a three-month intervention, so now the question we ask ourselves is what improvement would we have seen in students' scores if we had continued the pilot project group for six or nine months? As in all good inquiry, action research, we continue to ask questions as we learn. Most important, we believe we have enough positive data to feel that SSR with Interventions is a valuable instructional strategy and an effective use of instructional time.

TODAY

Our action research has made a visible difference in our school.

During the 2005–2006 school year, I presented our results at a school staff meeting. As I shared what we did, the simple steps we followed, and the difference it made in reading comprehension and attitudes, the room grew absolutely silent. Have you ever been at a school staff meeting? At our meetings, there is always a smattering of side chatter, quiet conversations sparked by the current discussion. But this time, there was nothing. All eyes were on me, but nobody spoke. My fellow collaborators were available to answer questions, but nobody asked questions. I thought "uh-oh." I thought I had ruined our work by making a poor presentation. But what other staff members told me afterward was that our results had impressed them so much that it had caused speechlessness en masse. Throughout the next month, as staff members digested the information, we received positive and excited comments from all content areas.

Our 2006–2007 School Improvement Plan's (SIP) primary focus is reading. With the data to back it up, our SIP includes SSR with Interventions as an integral component. Developed into the SIP is a 25-minute "advisory" time built into the middle of the school day for schoolwide participation in SSR with Interventions. I am chair of a schoolwide SSR committee and along with classroom teachers from a range of content areas, the committee is responsible for providing an implementation plan, staff training and support. We did it! We completed an action research project, we shared our results, and we influenced a positive schoolwide change.

REFERENCES

Bishop, Kay. *Connecting Libraries with Classrooms: The Curricular Roles of the Media Specialist.* Washington, OH: Linworth, 2003.

Hatfield, Dr. James. E-mail message to author. 16 May 2005.

———. E-mail message to author. 7 March 2006.

———. E-mail message to author. 21 August 2006.

Indiana Department of Education. "Indiana Accountability System for Academic Progress (ASAP)." 2005. http://www.doe.state.in.us/asap/welcome.html. (Accessed 30 March 2006).

———. "ISTEP+ InfoCenter." 2005. http://www.doe.state.in.us/istep/2005/welcome.html. (Accessed 2 April 2006)

———. "Statewide ISTEP+ Results Show Gains in Math; Modest Improvements in English/Language Arts and Science." IDE News Release. 22 December 2005. http://www.doe.state.in.us/reed/newsr/2005/12-December/ISTEPresults.html. (Accessed 2 April 2006).

Krashen, Stephen. "Is In-School Free Reading Good for Children? Why the National Reading Panel Is (Still) Wrong," *Phi Delta Kappan* 86 (6): 444–447 (2005).

———. *The Power of Reading: Insights from the Research.* 2d ed. Westport, CT: Libraries Unlimited, 2004.

National Reading Panel. "Teaching Children to Read: An Evidence-Based Assessment of the Scientific Research Literature on Reading and Its Implications for Reading Instruction." NIH Publication No. 00–4754. 2000. http://www.nichd.nih.gov/publications/nrp/report.htm. (Accessed 1 February 2006).

"School Improvement Plan: NCA/P.L. 221/NCLBA." Perry Meridian Middle School. 1 May 2005.

"School Improvement Plan: NCA/P.L. 221/NCLBA." Perry Meridian Middle School. May 2006.

3

SSR with
Interventions Program

I know that the only way students will get better at reading, writing, and thinking is if they actually read, write, and think.

—Tovani (2004)

Included in this chapter are fundamentals for implementing an SSR with Interventions program, as well as elements intended to enhance the program. Enriching the program will allow it to grow and meet the needs of developing readers as teachers become comfortable and competent in what may be a new role for the secondary educator. It is simple. Keep it simple. Once those involved see how simple it is, you can add supporting pieces that enhance the experience.

IMPLEMENTING SUSTAINED SILENT READING WITH INTERVENTIONS

SSR with Interventions can be implemented at the classroom, team, grade, or building level. If a grade or building level, enlist a core group of teacher-leaders to help guide, model, and train others. Include on the committee an administrator, school library media specialist, classroom teacher from an appropriate range of subject areas, and if your situation permits, a student from each grade level and a parent representative.

As with all good things implemented in schools, it takes ongoing attention and teacher commitment to properly implement the program. Once the routine is established, it is as easy to maintain as any other classroom routine. As Elizabeth Sweeney stated, "Some time was required to get students into the pattern of finding notebooks, reading material, etc. Students resisted at first but became increasingly cooperative as the semester continued. At the conclusion of the SSR project, students were able to enter the classroom, obtain materials, and settle into quiet reading with little prompting."

Figure 3.1. SSR with Interventions Student, Classroom Teacher, Committee, Library Media Specialist, Administrator Roles

---

Students

Before — Upon entering the room . . .

- Follow the classroom teacher's established routine for distributing reading-writing-response journals. Read any note left in journal by the teacher.
- Find reading material.
- Read prompt.

During — Read every day . . .

- Three to four days are self-selected reading from any material with a plot (novel, graphic novel, short story, fairy tale, folk tale, etc.).
- One to two days are teacher-selected informational text (magazine/newspaper article, map, manual, recipe, directions, website, primary document, etc.).
- Supplement reading participation with teacher directed reading promotion activities.

After — At the conclusion of SSR time . . .

- Responds to the day's reading and the teacher-selected prompt in the student's reading-writing-response journal.

Classroom Teachers

Before — Prior to SSR . . .

- Select a prompt appropriate for that day.
- Write prompt in designated location on board or overhead before SSR begins so students can see it and think about it as they read.

During — SSR with Interventions

- Start SSR by modeling good reading behavior and read with students during the first few minutes.
- After a few minutes, once the class has settled into SSR, conference with individual student about his or her reading (divide class into the days of the week and conference with the number of students each day necessary for all students to receive a personal student-teacher reading conference by end of the week).
- When SSR time is over and students are writing in their reading-writing-response journal, complete Teacher Observation Log and write notes about students in Teacher Conference Log.
- Supplement reading with creative choices for reading promotion: audio book, group sharing, paired reading, read-aloud, recommendations, skill building, student-led sharing, and think-alouds.

After — Post-SSR . . .

- Read student's reading-writing-response journals (divide class into the days of the week and review the number of journals each day necessary for all students to receive a personal comment in their journals by end of the week).
- Make positive comments/personal connection related to something in student's reading-writing-response journal on a sticky note. Hang note out of journal for student to easily find and read the next day.

Committee

- Locate and distribute informational text selections (magazine/newspaper article, map, manual, recipe, directions, Web site, primary document, etc.) and accompanying prompt choices.

An overview of recommended SSR with Interventions participant roles outlines steps to emulate the program.

Figure 3.1. (Continued)

Library Media Specialist
- Incorporate reading promotion strategies into annual plan, including keeping staff, students, and parents informed about new fiction and non-fiction.
- Work with committee to schedule and present staff how-to training reading promotion: audio book, group sharing, paired reading, read-aloud, recommendations, skill building, student-led sharing, and think-alouds.
- Prepare and promote state, national, themed, and genre reading lists.
- Attend trainings and conferences related to reading motivation, new literature, and reading comprehension strategies.

Administrator
- Advocate, promote and monitor SSR with Interventions.
- Foster a reading culture and climate.

School's Role

With a basic instructional plan and a few fundamental tools, SSR with Interventions can be implemented in a school or classroom. Figure 3.1 outlines the program basics and participant roles. Figure 3.2 lists the few, simple supplies necessary for school or classroom implementation of SSR with Interventions.

Classroom Teacher Commitment

The classroom teacher is on the front line in the attempt to encourage and foster reading to the point that students view reading as commonplace and an established norm. Without the commitment, support, and meaningful participation of the classroom teacher, SSR with Interventions cannot gain the momentum required to be successful.

Classroom teachers must be willing to consider SSR time and activities sacred. Once begun, give it the support it deserves for the duration and continue the program throughout the year. Students must be able to rely and depend upon the structure and stability

Figure 3.2. SSR with Interventions Supplies

- ✓ A classroom bookshelf and school library media center well stocked with up-to-date and popular stories and informational texts.
- ✓ Reading-writing-response journal for each student.
- ✓ Place to keep reading-writing-response journal in classroom.
- ✓ Generic writing prompts.
- ✓ Informational texts and companion prompt.
- ✓ Sticky notes for teacher comments in student's reading-writing-response journal.
- ✓ Binder or folders for classroom teacher to keep Teacher Observation Log and Teacher Conference Log materials organized.

Just a few supplies are necessary for school or classroom implementation of SSR with Interventions.

of continuity. During a regular school day, do not veer from the regimen and routine of the established SSR time and events. Nina Phagan, seventh-grade Language Arts teacher, states: "Many kids do not have routine and structure at home, and yet they need it. As a teacher, if I do not provide stability in the lives of my students (in my classroom) I cannot possibly begin to expect them to eventually move beyond SSR reading to become stable lifelong readers. This stability and structure of a regular reading routine proves to my kids that reading is important in school and beyond. Nothing is more important or worth replacing our SSR time. If we don't read, if we don't keep our routine, I am telling the kids that reading is only important *some* of the time."

Library Media Specialist Commitment

The library media specialist is one of the building reading experts. She is skilled with reading promotion techniques, some of which are suggested in this chapter and Chapter 4. The library media specialist is an anchor, cheerleader, moral support person, and advocate for SSR. The library media specialist has a unique perspective of the entire school and is a building specialist on literature, reading strategies, reading promotion, teacher training, school climate, and student literacies. Use this to instructional advantage. Make the most of the professional skills of the building's library media specialist. According to fifth-grade teacher Jim Preddy: "The classroom teacher is restricted to their immediate classroom/learning community and may not be aware of what's going on in the whole building. The media specialist has the unique advantage of being aware of what's going on in various classrooms, grade levels, learning communities and can match up strategies that work with struggling classrooms. They can work with individual teachers as well as individual students that may be overwhelmed."

Taking advantage of the library media specialist's talents is as efficient as using monthly school faculty meetings as an opportunity to introduce, model, and train staff on new elements, provide booktalks, share community reading resources and programs, etc. This is a prime opportunity for the library media specialist to slip into the role of reader's advisor for classroom teachers (Zimmerman 2005). It would be helpful for the library media specialist to regularly check in or conference with classroom teachers to find out how they're doing and what the library media specialist could do to help. Often a classroom teacher will not seek out assistance, but once the library media specialist initiates the discussion, thoughts and feelings are often freely expressed.

Administrator Commitment

Although SSR can be accomplished without the wholehearted support of the building administration, administration support increases its potential and longevity. As in all things in the school, the administrator is the barometer for success in the building. The administrator sets the climate in which students, teachers, and parents co-exist. Administrator support can be represented in many forms and levels: verbal approval of classroom-level participation, visual support through modeling, written support through parent communications and/or the school improvement plan, curricular support by incorporating schoolwide SSR into the daily schedule, and financial support through consistent funding of the school library media center and classroom bookshelves.

Excellent administrators regularly engage students, parents, and staff in casual conversation. This is a way to keep his finger on the pulse of his microcosm of society, the school. A standard aspect of these informal discussions should include dialogue about books and reading. What better way to establish a community of literacy than to have the building leadership express reading importance by giving time to expressing interest through personal conversations?

Sustained Silent Reading

SSR is remarkably simple to implement and sustain. It takes educator commitment, student reading resources, and time. It is startling that something so easy to fund and support as SSR isn't in every school in the nation. Is it because it seems too simple to be true? Is it because of our human nature demanding a more challenging solution to the complex problems of student reading comprehension? SSR with Interventions proves the difficult route is not the one needed. A well-rounded reading comprehension program, aimed at building a community of readers, incorporates SSR as an integral piece of the instructional puzzle.

Logistics

Establish approximately 20 to 25 minutes per day for SSR with Interventions. When the program is implemented throughout the building, this provides 15 to 20 minutes for reading and 3 to 5 minutes for responding to the reading prompt in the reading-writing-response journal. At the secondary level, 20 to 25 minutes is a prime number for SSR. Less time and students aren't given enough time to become absorbed by what they are reading; more time and students become restless. It is also a length of time that isn't difficult to carve out of the instructional day. Cut as little as 30 to 60 seconds off passing periods and 2 minutes from each instructional period to establish a special SSR period for the school day. If faculty would like to increase that time to more than 25 minutes, consider the need to slowly build a student's reading endurance. The amount of time a student can concentrate and stay focused on the reading task may be limited. Start with 25 minutes, adding five minutes every two to six weeks until the desired amount of time and reader stamina is reached.

If the program is implemented independently in the classroom, it is possible to get by with as little as 15 minutes SSR and 3 minutes journaling, depending on how long class periods are in the school. The longer the class period, the closer to 20 minutes can be achieved. Begin the period with SSR. If the class period's routine is instituted properly, the established routine and structure will allow for more to be accomplished than was thought possible with the instructional time left. As Howard Ely, seventh-grade Science teacher, declared, "I have used SSR at the beginning of the class period for many months and have found that it gets the students quiet, and immediately focused on learning … they are more ready to get into the classwork and seem to be more mentally awake." See Figure 3.3 for an overview of SSR with Interventions.

Permit students a great deal of latitude and choice when selecting reading material. For free choice days, allow anything with a plot to be read (that is not assigned reading for a class). If the student does not have something of his own, allow him to bring something from the school library media center or borrow from the classroom bookshelf.

Figure 3.3.   Implementing SSR with Interventions in Your School

- SSR every school day as part of the school day or class period routine.
- Each SSR session lasts 20 to 25 minutes.
  - Spend 15 to 20 minutes reading.
  - Spend 3 to 5 minutes journaling.
- Self-selected reading, material with a plot, three times a week.
- Because state standardized proficiency tests deal with literature and informational text, spend one to two days per week using magazine article, newspaper article, instruction manual, map, directions, Web resource, booklet, brochure, etc.
- Except for classroom teacher selected informational text day, all other reading should be material with a plot and student choice.
- Incorporate promoting reading with students. Do this by devoting one day a week to reading promotion strategies or integrate it into extra time on informational text days.
- Establish a routine and procedures for SSR in the classroom. Do not break from that routine.
- Post the reading-writing prompt prior to the beginning of SSR.
- Hold individual conversations with students during SSR daily (rotating so each student has a personal conversation with the classroom teacher once a week, or as frequently as possible).
- When not holding student-teacher reading conference, classroom teacher should model by reading.
- Maintain a place in the classroom to keep the student reading-writing-response journals.
- Write a personal response in each student's journal once a week (rotating so each student has a personal note from the classroom teacher once a week).
- Do NOT grade the journals or correct conventions.
- Keep a teacher SSR journal that includes the date, reading-writing prompt used, anecdotal records, and description of conversations with students.
- Maintain an observation checklist daily.

The routine of SSR with Interventions is easy to duplicate in any classroom.

Do not allow the selection of reading material to bog down the program or for a student to use it as a crutch for failure. Help students work through the first few weeks of implementation by not allowing them to fail at reading selection. If they cannot come prepared, be prepared for them with a selection of short stories from which to choose. Once the routine is set, educator expectations have been made apparent, and a students' self-fulfilling obstacle of habitually being unprepared is eliminated, students will fall in step with the program. At first students may begin participating because the classroom teacher gives them no choice. The goal is for students to eventually commit themselves because time spent reading has become enjoyable.

Model what is expected of students. Always have reading material on hand. Begin SSR by reading while the students read. Make selections similar to the students: free choice. Make a conscious choice to read adult as well as popular adolescent material.

Once SSR reading time is in full swing with all students engaged in reading, set the reading aside. Begin conferencing the selected students for that day. If conferences are complete and reading time is still available, pick the material back up and continue reading until SSR time is over. After SSR, while students are responding to the prompt in their reading-writing-response journal, write notes related to the student conferences in a teacher SSR journal. Use the sample teacher observation log in Chapter 6 to keep track of student participation and to track the conferencing and reading of student journals. When time allows throughout the day, read and leave sticky note comments in the day's selected student journals.

Material with a Plot

Three to four days a week ask students to select reading material with a plot. This includes novels, short stories, story collections, plays, graphic novels, picture books, fairy tales, folk tales, myths, legends, etc. Anything with a plot, at any length, will do. Limit it to material with a plot so that students can hone skills required to follow a plot to fruition. A plot requires following character development, setting, themes, story elements, etc. Many students need this opportunity to build endurance and to practice the stick-to-it-ness sometimes necessary to plod through a difficult section of a good reading.

Informational Text

Jean Donham (1998) defines three purposes to reading: "reading for literary experience, reading for information, and reading to perform a task" (p. 144). It is estimated that 80 percent of secondary standardized test questions are related to informational text passages (Cornwell and Gillespie 2004). Because of the focus standardized tests have on comprehending informational text, allow time each week to focus on informational text, which covers the latter two purposes described by Donham. With educator assistance, students gain practice reading for a purpose, which is the key to unlocking the ability to manipulate informational text. To make this easier on everyone participating in SSR with Interventions, use the committee to aid in the location of informational text material. Informational text comes in many forms: an article from a magazine, newspaper, or Web site; manual; catalog; sales flyer; Web page; nonfiction passage; directions; recipe; pamphlet; menu; food label; song lyrics; map; etc. With the committee's help, timely, high interest material and material related to what is being promoted schoolwide or by a grade level can be located and shared with suggested writing prompts.

BUILDING STUDENT-TEACHER RELATIONSHIPS

A key reason that SSR with Interventions is effective is because of the personal relationship built between the student and the SSR teacher. Educator strategies necessary for building comprehension and fluency are progress monitoring and modeling (Millikan 2003). Student progress is monitored through student conferencing, responding to student reading-writing-response journals and maintaining a teacher SSR journal. Modeling strategies include reading aloud with correct punctuation and pace, openly discussing books and other readings, sharing reading enthusiasm.

Don't look for students to provide or share the right answer or interpretation. Instead, focus on building the relationship and trust. That is about what Jim Ellsberry calls "a conspiracy of caring" (1998, p. 3). Without emotional commitment, learning and participation from both teachers and students won't last.

Once the relationship reaches the trust level for a student to recommend something to a classroom teacher or the library media specialist, make every effort to read it or something similar by that author, then share with the student that you read it and what connections you made.

Student Reading-Writing-Response Journal

Students maintain a reading-writing-response journal. Callison and Preddy (2006) put forth the case for reading and writing being activities linked to skills necessary to establish reading/writing purpose and in the learners' ability to process meaning. This is a tool educators have used when I was a student and similar to what Short et al. (1996, p. 469) call "literature logs," Robb (2000, p. 266) terms a "response journal," Olson (2003, p. 107) identifies as a "reader response log," Smith and Wilhelm (2002, p. 206) name a "reading log," Fountas and Pinnell (2001, p. 169) describe as a "reader's notebook," or Tovani's (2004, p. 110) "reading response log," etc. It is as simple as a steno pad, a 4 × 6 inch spiral-bound notebook, a three-ring binder, a file folder, a composition book, or a teacher-created booklet with enough pages to get through a grading period, semester, or year. Middle school students love to doodle, so allow them to personalize and decorate the journal cover. These journals are to always remain in the classroom. Keep them in a designated location in the classroom, which will aid in establishing the daily routine.

The initial page of the journal includes the student's name, SSR teacher's name, and maybe even areas for an ongoing list of favorite books, Web sites, authors, subjects, themes, and genres. Each day's entry begins with the date, title, pages read, reading-writing prompt, and student's response. Sample reading-writing-response journal templates can be found in Chapter 6.

In the first days of SSR with Interventions use a simple writing prompt and allow extra time for processing the prompt response. The classroom teacher models on a board or presentation tool with talk-aloud strategies as she writes and a sample written response is formed.

Student reading-writing-response journals are private. Allow journal entries to be expressive. Give students the security that comes with an understanding that nobody will read the contents but the SSR teacher and the reader.

Reading-Writing Prompts

Create prompts or choose from the list of generic prompts found in Chapter 5. A prompt might require a student to create a graphic organizer, sketch, or write a paragraph of post-reading thoughts and reflections. Progressively move students beyond the basic read and reflect and into personal insights and connections to events and the world around them.

Before SSR begins, display the prompt in a prominent location in the classroom. Use that location, which can be as simple as writing and displaying from the overhead or dedicating a section of the classroom chalkboard or white board, consistently. Posting the prompt for students to view before reading begins gives students an opportunity to focus and create a reading purpose. Additionally, students thrive on feeling they have some freedom of choice; consider providing two prompts instead of one, then allowing the student to pick the one that best speaks to him.

Initially, expect students to use the prompt you provide. As the reader progresses, allow him to step away from the teacher-prescribed prompt to his own intrinsic and reflective inquiry. Allowing this freedom requires a closer monitoring of student reading-writing-response journals. A student may occasionally feel moved to write related to his epiphany-like reading experience. The problem would arise with the student who decides to do his own thing every time or is not a mature enough reader to reflect on his reading on his own as effectively as he would with the teacher's guided prompt.

Student-Teacher Reading Conference

Conferencing with students has two purposes: building a relationship between student and educator and assisting the educator in getting to know the reader. Each student receives a personal, one-on-one conference with the SSR teacher each week. Fountas and Pinnell (2001) explain that "A reading conference is not an interrogation. The questions you ask need to be genuine questions. You are treating the student as a reader. An onlooker would probably observe two people engaged in lively conversation about a book" (p. 123). Be a good listener and try to listen with an open heart. A simple way to show the student you are listening and to draw him further into the conversation is to ask your initial question, then allow something the student said to direct your next question. Students may be hesitant to speak at first and the educator will need take care while developing a personal relationship built on reading and trust. Robb (2000) states, "What you and I say to a student … reverberates and replays in their minds for a long time—in some cases, a lifetime" (p. 114). Figure 3.4 provides basic discussion concepts appropriate for initiating a reading discussion.

To make meeting with all students each week as simple and convenient for the classroom teacher as possible, take the number of students in class and divide by the days of the school week. Conference with the calculated number of students each day to ensure all students get their deserved time with the SSR teacher each week. Mix things up every week so the same student doesn't quickly become jaded to the realization that Monday is his day. There should be no routine for when each student receives his conference or the relationship will never mature. If the classroom teacher makes this routine, student will begin to see it as just another requirement instead of a true interest in his thoughts, feelings, opinions, and experiences. Each conference usually takes only a few worthwhile minutes. Eighth grade Algebra and Geometry teacher, Stephanie Quinlan, emphasizes, "I got to know the students a lot better because of the one-on-one conferences. Some students seem the quiet-do-everything-right kind of kid, but like to read unexpected books … I wouldn't have known this in a regular classroom setting."

Be flexible. If a student is absent or called out of the classroom on the day you expected to conference him, substitute another student in his place. If there is a particular day of the week that a student tends to be absent from the classroom, adjust the weekly conference schedule around that anticipated conflict. If a particular student needs more conference time than usual, give him that time and adjust the week's conferencing schedule accordingly. If the classroom teacher cannot conference with every student within the week, reach as many students as possible. Spending sincere time with each individual is more important that keeping to a schedule.

Teacher SSR Journal

Classroom teacher notes can be kept in a three-ring class binder, with an opening section for miscellaneous information, then a divider separating each student's information, or kept in individual pocket or file folders for each student.

Figure 3.4. Book Discussion Concepts

- Author's impact on story
- Cause/Effect
- Character
  - conflicts
    - nature
    - self
    - others
  - methods of dealing
- Compare/Contrast
  - Situations
    - in book
    - with similar books
    - with us
- Comprehension
- Difficult Situations
- Experiences
- Feelings of
  - author
  - reader
  - character
- Mood
  - what is the mood
  - affect on characters
  - affect on reader
- Plot
  - problem
  - turning point
  - solution
- Theme

Consider basic book discussion concepts appropriate for initiating a reading discussion.

Include in the journal a daily entry for the SSR date, time spent reading, and writing prompt used. Once the enrichments have begun, include in the log the enrichment tool used and title, author, and location of material shared. Make note of students exhibiting off-task behavior (not reading) during SSR and journal notes related to student conferences. Sample classroom teacher conference and observation logs to use for this purpose are in Chapter 6.

Keep anecdotal records of student-teacher reading conference conversations with students. A quick way to add important personal information to the student's conference log is to use a sticky note to add personal facts as you learn them. Keeping these anecdotal records may help the classroom teacher know that child as an individual. As the classroom teacher begins to know the student, it becomes easier to recommend reading material.

Teacher Observation Log

An important concern to be addressed is keeping kids on-task during SSR. Maintaining an observation log to monitor student reading behavior and track the weekly conferencing schedule is helpful. It allows the classroom teacher to track student behavior and monitor for patterns and changes in behavior. Getting to know the student personally and monitoring patterns of behavior allows the classroom teacher to develop personalized effective intervention strategies. A sample teacher observation log is available in Chapter 6.

Teacher Conference Log

Wait to begin conferencing until students have settled into the classroom routine and expectations and the educator no longer needs to take extra time to model quiet and focused reading. Use conferencing time to look for evidence of the student's thinking while reading, to build a personal relationship with the student, and to help build his reading confidence. Candy Schaefer, seventh grade Language Arts teacher, stated, "It was surprising to find that some students didn't actually realize how their reading had changed until I discussed their reading with them. After each discussion they were excited when they realized they had become a better reader, there was also an increase in class participation in reading aloud."

Until the educator gains comfort and confidence in the process, conferencing can be as simple as asking the student the day's prompt and listening to his response. Once instructional confidence is gained, branch out and allow for more conversational freedoms. Have the student read-aloud a page of what he is reading, and then discuss it or problems the student had with it. Have the student share reading moods, emotions, personal issues, or connections from text to self, the world, or other text.

Once SSR has concluded and journal time has begun, as the students write in their reading-writing-response journal, take that time to write notes about the student conferences held. Include personal observations and anecdotes for the day. A sample teacher conference log is available in Chapter 6.

ACCESS TO BOOKS

For students to develop or maintain an interest in reading and eventually become a lifelong reader, they need to be surrounded by books at school and home. School libraries and classroom bookshelves need to include up-to-date, fashionable, and quality reading material. This encompasses all genres, themes, and formats of fiction and nonfiction, or other informational texts. Include grade-level text, high interest-low vocabulary for students reading below grade level, and high interest-high vocabulary for students reading above grade level. If unsure where to start, or wishing to begin with established lists, try recommendation lists found in professional journals, books, and Web sites. Some great Web sites to try are:

Jon Scieszka's GUYS READ™	www.guysread.com
Middle Grades Reading Network High Interest/ Low Readability Books and High Interest/High Readability Books	http://mgrn.evansville.edu/index.asp
YALSA Young Adult Services Association Booklists and BookAwards	http://www.ala.org/yalsa/booklists

Figure 3.5.   The Reader's Triad

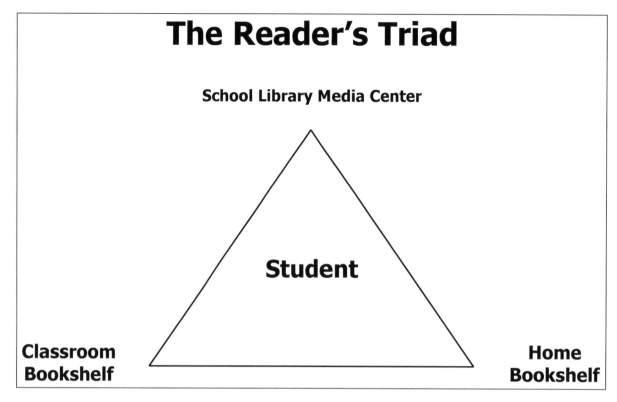

Schools need to help surround students with reading material. An effective reader has free access to voluntary reading materials in the home, library media center, and classroom.

School Library Media Center

Students need open and frequent access to a library media center well stocked with trendy topics and literature. If your library media center has the space to do so, allow for what I call Self-Selected Reading checkout time. Our media center has seating capacity for multiple classrooms, so we can have a teacher-library media specialist collaborative research project going on and a full class coming in to check out books. It works well for us to schedule Language Arts classes in a 20-minute block once a week for Self-Selected Reading checkout. Classes enter the media center and students are expected to look for something to check out or, if the student isn't ready to exchange books, find a place to read quietly.

That library media center should include a library media specialist. The library media specialist is integral to keeping up with the trends in children's literature and is vital to connecting kids to books. Mary Jane Jones, a high school library media specialist, expounds, "When it comes to reading, the library media specialist is the Who knows the Hows of reading instruction and guides toward the Whats. What are the Whats? The Whats are the wide variety of materials that kids read and helping kids find the Whats they want without judging their selections. (I gladly accept the blame for giving a high school girl a book that she read under the covers by the light on her alarm clock. I gladly accept the blame for the guy who locked himself in the bathroom and ran water in the sink so his family would not hear him crying while he finished reading a book.) Library media specialists know about graphic language, graphic arts, and graphic novels. We know about the science of dreams, the dream careers, the nightmares of disease, and the dreams and nightmares of the people in fiction and biography. We connect with the kids so they can connect with their dreams and fears through books."

Classroom Bookshelves

It is ideal for each classroom to have a classroom bookshelf of student pleasure-reading materials that include fiction and up-to-date informational texts. Find a place to keep the classroom bookshelf: shelf, crate, or cubby. These books should be a free-fault zone. They shouldn't be cataloged or inventoried and don't worry about the books disappearing—consider each lost book a reader found.

Each classroom should have a collection of around 50 to 75 books. Less than 50 books and there isn't enough variety. Much more than 75 books and students become so overwhelmed with so many choices they have difficulty finding something to read. If there are more than 100 books, consider organizing them in a way that makes sense to students. Or take the advice my children's pediatrician gave me about toddler toys, which also applies to classroom bookshelves: keep only a portion of the books on the shelf. Box up the rest or return them to the SSR Lending Library. Every grading period, rotate books off the shelf and replace them with the previously stored books. This collection should continually change and evolve, so try to curb the desire to personalize each book with classroom teacher name or room number. Instead just stamp the book as property of the school and any time a book is found or returned, it can be placed on a community bookshelf for classroom teachers to take from as they need. There are ideas in Chapter 4 for how to continually keep the classroom bookshelf selection fresh with an SSR Lending Library.

Students need to be surrounded by books. There should be a bookshelf in every classroom, not just the Language Arts classroom. For a classroom bookshelf to be effective, it must be supplemented with a healthy, well-stocked, professionally staffed library media center. A classroom bookshelf does not take the place of a school library media center, but is instead one aspect necessary for surrounding students with reading material and building a community of readers. My school's library media center circulation statistics continue to increase as classroom bookshelves have been instituted. Access to books establishes a reading climate and a community of readers. The more frequent access to books, the more reading occurs. Both pieces are necessary to meet the demanding task of creating lifelong readers.

Home Bookshelves

Ideally, all students would come from a home where reading is modeled and encouraged, and a plethora of reading materials are available, but that isn't always the situation. The SSR Committee works together to brainstorm ideas to get books into students' hands. Host a public library card drive at student orientation and back to school night. Award kids caught doing good deeds with a book. Reward PTA fundraiser participants with a magazine subscription. Student incentive for good behavior, meeting goals, etc., is the prize of a book to add to their home bookshelves, instead of pizza parties and prize tokens. There are many other ideas the committee could dream up to help students establish or expand a personal home library.

READING PROMOTION

Another part of SSR with Interventions is reading promotion. Consider substituting SSR for time spent sharing reading experiences or use informational text days, when the informational text doesn't take as long as the allotted SSR time. As your competence and confidence grows, begin to delve into some of the reading promotion suggestions listed here, or other suggestions generated by your building's educators or your school's SSR Committee.

Don't try to implement all of the additional tools and techniques at once—wait until you and your staff are comfortable with one element before trying another. I compare it to when I started my job and everything seemed overwhelming. I often wondered how, if ever, I would get through the school year and accomplish all the tasks I, or others, expected of me. Once I realized I needed to take one responsibility at a time, become proficient at it, then add another until I became proficient at it, and keep moving on, everything came together and was more manageable. Take the same view with reading promotion. Figure 3.6 provides the basic outline of things to keep to in mind when promoting reading.

When selecting material to promote, confirm that copies are available to students through the library media center. A resistive or struggling reader would consider it unforgivable if something is advertised, but he doesn't have access to it.

Audio "Book"

Borrow from the school library or public library engaging text to audio material. Choose well-done quality audios. Listening to good audio books model for the educator and student effective and entertaining material being read aloud by professional orators

Figure 3.6. Reading Promotion Basics

1. Know your audience. Play to social trends, personal interests, and local and global current issues.
2. The more you do while the reading material is fresh in your mind, the better.
3. Be familiar with the material. Be interested in the material.
4. Like the material. If you're not sure, get references. Consult professional journals, book reviews, books that review and recommend other books; consult others in your school or profession who enjoy that type of reading material.
5. Never tell the ending. Telling the ending removes much of the intrigue necessary for a reader's mind to become interested.
6. Share a personal anecdote: why did the reading appeal to you?
7. Include interesting facts from the reading that help set the mood and theme.
8. Find brief passages or quotes that you liked.
9. Find the "hook"—what "caught" your attention that you should share with the audience.
10. Find a place to keep notes, which could be a folder on your computer, a box of index cards, or a 3-ring binder. Take notes on what you plan to say and do; make changes afterward to adjust to what you would do differently next time.

Ten reminders for promoting reading most effectively.

and actors. It is not necessary to listen to the complete recording. Select an especially engaging section that ends on a cliff-hanger to motivate the student to read the rest on his own.

"Book"-Talk

Introduce a suggested reading to students through a teasing, and yet informative, talk. Talk material with a plot as well as informational text. Give students a reason to want to read it without giving away too much, including the ending. Revisit Figures 3.4 and 3.6 for helpful hints.

Group Sharing

Model for students how to share reading enthusiasm. As a class or in small groups, share material that is being read and enjoyed. Let the students share in discussions about free choice readings. Select prompts found in Chapter 5 for discussion starters until students grow proficient enough to initiate and generate dialogue independently.

Paired Reading

Allow students to practice the read-aloud skills being modeled by educators. Pair up students. Prepare students in advance for this upcoming opportunity; give them the opportunity to review reading material and select what they consider engaging passages, phrases, sections, or stanzas worth sharing with others. Partner students for the most effective groupings. Have students use the occasion to share why they selected a certain piece and what it means to them, and then to read to their respective partners the chosen piece.

Read-Aloud or "Tease" Reading

Read-aloud to students a moving, entertaining, powerful, or informative passage from a novel, article, anthology, short story, poetry, picture book, Web site, student work, informational text, etc. Oral interpretation, more casually known as reading aloud, is done with enthusiasm, inflection, and heart, even when what's being read is informational text. My five-year-old daughter has begun to really enjoy being read to, but will bluntly tell me if I've done a poor job. As we turned the last page, she once took the book out of my hand, turned back to page one, handed it back to me and said, "Do it again, but do it right this time." My daughter was willing to say what students will only usually express with body language, which is that reading out loud to someone requires one to read aloud with purpose and passion. Don't turn kids off by using the infamous monotone. Instead use this as an opportunity to model for students how to read with interest and emotion. Don't be afraid to be cheesy or use props. Make personal connections to the selection and stop at times to ask questions or to explain your thinking. As Alison Hart said, "[T]hey would *beg* me to read to them." Keep trying until you've found your read-aloud voice to engage your audience and capture their internal imagination.

Don't avoid picture books—use them! Picture books are great for reading aloud to older children. A person is never too old for picture books, and there are many picture books written for older readers. There are other picture books that are great for reading aloud because they evoke memories in the students from when they read it or it was read to them when they were younger. For example, my middle school students continue to enjoy Dr. Seuss, Chris Van Allsburg, David Shannon, Maurice Sendak, Ian Falconer, and more. There are other picture books with mature subject matter intended for an older audience. For example, *That Summer* (Harcourt, 2002) by Tony Johnston and illustrated by Barry Moser is about a family, including a dying child, that puts together a quilt of love and memories as they deal with the impending death. *Michael Rosen's Sad Book* (Candlewick, 2004) illustrated by Quentin Blake conveys deep emotions as the author deals with soul darkening sadness.

Recommendations

Introduce a suggested reading to students through a recommendation. Propose material with a plot as well as informational text. Discuss why you found it interesting and worth sharing. Explain what you know about the student that made you think he would be interested. Connect to students' lives. Share a personal anecdote about how you found it or how you found it connects to your own life. Share more about the whys than you actually share about the specific details of the recommended reading. If you are unsure what to recommend, describe the reader's interests to somebody fluent in adolescent literacy, like the library media specialist, and ask for guidance. The student will be impressed that you cared enough to get advice on his behalf.

Skill Building

Use a piece of SSR time as an opportunity for skill building. Incorporate a reading skill minilesson. Sample resources that could be guides for skill building lessons are on reproducible bookmarks in Chapter 6. Have the library media specialist, reading specialist/coordinator, or other expert on reading in the building share at a staff meeting a reading strategy and minilesson for the staff to incorporate into a skill-building SSR day. This training will help guide content area teachers and other educators without a reading teaching background. John Hagenmaier, seventh and eighth grade Social Studies teacher, considers developing reading skills important: "Content-area teachers who assume that only reading teachers can and should teach reading are wrong. Simple strategies that model questioning and connecting to prior knowledge can easily be taught by anyone."

Student-Led Sharing

Allow for a day when students can share with the class something they've enjoyed reading and think others might enjoy too. This is an opportunity to talk through what was enjoyable and noteworthy. Share enthusiasm and encourage others to try reading it as well. This allows students an opportunity to get actively involved in building a community of readers by advertising reading to others. Refer to Figure 3.6 for guidelines, some of which could be adapted for student use.

Think-Aloud

Read-aloud to students while pausing to verbalize strategies you use to understand, think about, and absorb the text. For example, thinking about what you already know, connecting to yourself or someone you know, sounding out a word that is not familiar, asking questions before, during, and after reading, finding an answer in the text to a question you'd previously asked yourself are some think-aloud strategies.

REFERENCES

Callison, Daniel, and Leslie Preddy. *The Blue Book on Information Age Inquiry, Instruction and Literacy.* Westport, CT: Libraries Unlimited, 2006.

Cornwell, Linda, and Julie Gillespie. "Reading Comprehension: The Bridge to Information Literacy." Workshop presentation at Scholastic Literacy Workshop, Indianapolis, IN, January 2004.

Donham, Jean. *Enhancing Teaching and Learning: A Leadership Guide for School Library Media Specialists.* New York: Neal-Schuman, 1998.

Ellsberry, Jim. "Twenty-One Teaching Methods for the Analogical Teacher's Classroom." Workshop presentation at the Metropolitan School District of Perry Township DeWitt Institute for Professional Development Seminar, Indianapolis, IN, July 1998.

Fountas, Irene C., and Gay Su Pinnell. *Guiding Readers and Writers: Teaching Comprehension, Genre, and Content Literacy.* Portsmouth, NH: Heinemann, 2001.

Johnston, Tony. *That Summer.* Illustrated by Barry Moser. San Diego, CA: Harcourt, 2002.

Millikan, Ann. "Read Naturally Strategy: Fluency and Comprehension." Presentation at Indiana State Reading Association Annual Conference, Indianapolis, IN, March 2003.

Olson, Carol Booth. *The Reading/Writing Connection: Strategies for Teaching and Learning in the Secondary Classroom.* Boston: Allyn and Bacon, 2003.

Robb, Laura. *Teaching Reading in Middle School.* New York: Scholastic, 2000.

Rosen, Michael. *Michael Rosen's Sad Book.* Illustrated by Quentin Blake. Cambridge, MA: Candlewick, 2004.

Short, Kathy G., et al. *Creating Classrooms for Authors and Inquirers.* 2nd ed. Portsmouth, NH: Heinemann, 1996.

Smith, Michael W., and Jeffrey D. Wilhelm. *"Reading Don't Fix No Chevys": Literacy in the Lives of Young Men.* Portsmouth, NH: Heinemann, 2002.

Tovani, Cris. *Do I Really Have to Teach Reading? Content Comprehension, Grades 6–12.* Portland, ME: Stenhouse, 2004.

Zimmerman, Nancy. "Research-Based Evidence: The Role of the Library Media Specialist in Reading Comprehension Instruction." *School Library Media Activities Monthly* 21 (9): 47–50 (2005).

4

The School Library Media Specialist Role: Building a Community of Readers

The LMS promotes, models, and empowers the success of all in making comprehension a school priority.

—McKenzie (2005)

The library media specialist is challenged with the task of keeping reading alive. She invites everyone in the school to the "literacy club" (Smith 1988). The school is its own mini-universe where every classroom is a planet, every home a star, and everything within this universe revolves around the life-giving sun, reading. It is the library media specialist's role to carry the torch and pass it on to classroom teachers and to give reading the light, warmth, and energy necessary to keep the universe alive and humming. To do this, the library media specialist must develop campaign strategies for promoting reading and keeping it in the heart, mind, and activity list of students, parents, and staff. Included in this chapter are programming ideas and suggestions that are not required for an SSR with Interventions program, but using some of these projects further enriches the success of the SSR experience for students and staff.

CREATING A COMMUNITY OF ADULT READERS

The first priority should be to establish a climate of adult readership. During adolescence, students may seem to view anything any adult in a school says or does as repulsive, but it is all just a façade. Students need to see us, all of us, as part of the great reading community. Support staff, teachers, and administrators all need to be led toward the light, to model what being a literate citizen is all about: reading, sharing, growing, and thinking. When a staff member carries a book around with her, keeps the current book she is reading on display, engages in reading conversations, and participates in reader activities, then the library media specialist knows she is doing a good job. When teachers lead by allowing students to see them reading and engaged in reading conversations and activities, students will follow. There are many ways to guide your school into a culture of readers; just a few are briefly described in the following pages.

Staff Meetings

Classroom teachers need to understand there is a wealth of good reading material written for tweens and teens. Odds are, though, that classroom teachers don't have the resources available to them that the library media specialist does. A library media specialist reads reviews, subscribes to e-newsletters, accesses annotated bibliographies, peruses Web sites, attends workshops and conferences, and has handfuls of magazines and newspapers pass through her fingers every month. The average classroom teacher does not have the opportunity for these experiences. Take the opportunity to them. Borrow a few minutes out of each staff meeting to tease and entice. Make it a goal to booktalk literature and informational text. Persuade them through your tantalizing conversations that their lives would not be complete without reading at least one of the items you share at the staff meeting. Adolescents need to see adult role models respecting their interests by reading things that they love to read. Once you talk staff into reading "kid stuff", they will find out how enjoyable it is and they will be addicted. They will experience how fun it is to be caught reading by students and engage students in literary conversations.

Secondary content area teachers may not understand how to promote reading or teach reading comprehension strategies: reading conferencing, modeling, think-aloud, booktalk, group sharing, paired reading, etc. Prepare in advance to partner with a classroom teacher or the SSR with Interventions committee to share with staff basic principles of a particular strategy. Model this strategy; one person taking on the role of student, one the role of educator. Research and develop a bookmark or handout with helpful tips that staff members can take away with them as a continual reminder of how to implement that strategy when working with students. Sample bookmarks are available in Chapter 6.

Give away adolescent literature to staff members at every possible moment. After giving a presentation at a staff meeting or training event, give out books as prizes or rewards. Staff may add the book to his classroom bookshelf and, hopefully, read it, be caught reading it, and share it with students.

Adult Lending Library

Staff won't be willing to spend all their time reading what the students read, so respect their adulthood. Create a no responsibility adult library, which doesn't cost anything to build. To begin, find a location in a library media center workroom, copy room, or other high-traffic staff area to designate as the Adult Lending Library. Once that is accomplished, place a bookshelf or book cart in that space, create a sign to place there to promote it, and ask staff for donations of adult reading material to begin the collection, fiction and nonfiction, with the understanding that not all donated books will be added to the adult lending library. The decision may be made not to add a book because the title is outdated, the collection already holds copies of that title, or the cover or content is not appropriate for in-school consumption by an influential adult authority figure. A few times a year remind teachers about the availability and location of the collection and ask for donations of adult reading material to add to the shelf. This collection is on the honor system, a no fault zone without barcodes or an official checkout procedure. If something isn't returned or damaged, no worries, it can be replaced with something else the next time there is a call for donations. Make that book part of its own promotion by creating labels to place on the covers, letting the reader and others watching the reader know that it came from your school's Adult Lending Library.

Teacher's Professional Collection

No school is complete without a professional collection for staff. Order a few new pieces a year related to the latest educational trends, research, and best practices. Include materials for all disciplines and grade levels, self-help, as well as information about adolescent behavior and learning. But don't stop there—this is just the beginning! As professional material enters the library media center, promote it. Put it on display in a high-traffic area. Include it in the staff newsletter. Booktalk or read aloud pieces at staff meetings. Invite staff to a breakfast, lunch, or after-school snack and sneak preview of the new items added to the professional collection. Create annotated bibliography bookmarks. While promoting these new items, try throwing in a few older pieces that deserve a second look or fit a theme.

Adult/Staff Book Club/Discussions

Everybody loves a party, so host parties, not another meeting! Send out invitations. Make your events special. Invite everyone! Provide snacks, drinks, and games. Mix it up so that you're not doing the same thing over and over again. And if something doesn't seem to go well, or attendance is low, don't give up. Ask around and find out what went wrong, then fix it for next time. If there seems to be nothing wrong with the planned event, then all it may take is doing it enough times that people get used to it and begin to expect the fun and camaraderie you have planned.

"White Elephant"

Host a book exchange party. Invite staff to bring a book they've read, enjoyed, and want to share with others. As people arrive, have them lay their books down in a designated area, get a snack while they socialize, and sneak a peek at the books brought to the party. While everyone is busy, sneak a bookmark, card, or note of some sort into one of the books. Once everyone has had a chance to look at the books on display, gather everyone together with their book, sitting in a circle. Whoever has the item that you hid in a book gets to start the game. She starts by sharing the book with the group. Working clockwise, continue until all people have shared. Once you're back to the beginning, the first person gets up and trades her book with another person, taking the book that most appealed to her. Continue this way, clockwise again, until all people have had a chance to trade. As in all "white elephant" parties, when it's a person's turn, she can trade for any book she wants, even one that had been already chosen. Have fun, learn about different books other people are reading, get a new book to read, and enjoy building relationships with co-workers.

Jig-Saw

It is often difficult keeping up with all the professional literature. Offer opportunities for staff members interested in reading about a particular professional topic or a specific professional book. Divide the chapters among those interested. Each person reads the assigned chapter and prepares to share it with the group. Give the group a week or two to do the pre-reading, then gather the group together to share their assigned sections. Participants could even create a bookmark, card, or other handout highlighting the finer points of their section. In this way, everyone gets the knowledge in just a fraction of the time and effort. Some books are written so that each chapter builds upon the previous chapter, so this activity does not work with every title. Read or skim the book in advance to assure the effectiveness of jig-sawing.

Professional Reading Meeting

A few times every school year there is an intriguing, monumental, or controversial educational publication. Invite faculty to read that material, and then join together for a discussion on what it means in education, to the school, to the classroom, to the teacher, to the student, to the parent, and to the community. These discussions are important because they help everyone broaden their horizons. First, it is a chance to discuss the reading's topic. Second, professionals join in the shared collective, hearing and learning from a variety of voices, perspectives, and life experiences.

There are also themes and trends that sweep through public education and it would behoove every educator to keep current of these themes and trends. As these topics begin to enter your region, peruse the professional literature and online databases for the latest, accurate, substantive resources on the topic. Once the school and local resources have been culled for material, narrow down the reading selection to those most valid, written by experts or groundbreakers in the field, and if possible, include conflicting perspectives. Invite faculty to participate. Allow each participant to select one piece from the reading choices, and then give a week or two to complete the reading. Once the group meets, allow each person to summarize her reading before opening up the meeting to the group for discussion and interpretation. Provide attendees with a bibliography of professional literature discussed, possibly even throwing in an addendum of a few items suggested for further reading. The addendum may include items you became aware of too late to use with the group or provide more in-depth coverage of the topic to guide further individual study.

Adult Literature

We don't always want to, nor do we have to, always read for a professional purpose. Building a school climate of readers includes adults being well-rounded readers as well, which encompasses reading to meet professional needs and reading adolescent and adult material. Find ways to develop a reading community among staff through adult literature promotion. Promote your city's "one book, one city" program. If your community doesn't have one, work with the public library or school district to develop one. Review popular reads in the staff newsletter. Coordinate a staff book club. Facilitate meetings after school to see the latest book-to-movie.

CREATING A COMMUNITY OF STUDENT READERS

Make reading a team sport. Frank Smith (1988) says educators need to help students join the "literacy club." He argues that, just as students want to join a club devoted to an activity they enjoy, being a reader and establishing a school climate of readership means joining others and wanting to join others in the "literacy club."

Access to Books

Students should see books handy at every turn. It becomes a natural extension of every classroom for students to feel comfortable browsing a classroom bookshelf, asking an adult's advice about what to read, and making regular visits to the library media center.

Access to reading material is vital to a developing reader. Arrange for each student/ team/class to receive weekly self-selected-reading and book-checkout time in the library media center. Approach classroom teachers/teams at the start of the year to schedule library media center self-selected-reading book-checkout time. This may not be a common practice in secondary schools, but it is effective. It won't take long before teachers will come to embrace and expect this opportunity for their students. Initially, develop a reader's rapport with the classroom teacher through casual discussion and modeling how to help students use the OPAC and develop other visual browse strategies. After the first visit or two of working together, the classroom teacher will have enough confidence to allow the library media specialist to step back and take care of other tasks or classes for instruction while the classroom teacher steps up and takes the lead. Whenever the library media specialist schedule permits, she may continue to assist these students and classes in their selection process, but the classroom teachers should always be there and maintain responsibility for the class. Maintaining responsibility allows the classroom teacher the opportunity to become more familiar with student reading interests, reading trends, the library media center collection, as well as encourage students at the right maturation moment to branch out and experience new reading interests.

SSR Lending Library

Encourage classroom bookshelves through a no fault revolving collection of paperbacks. Work with staff and administration to find a space in a room, closet, or workroom to store the SSR Lending Library. Once a location has been designated, fill that space with books faculty can borrow, return (or maybe never return), and exchange for their classroom bookshelf. Start-up may take some money and effort, but after that, it's nearly effortless to maintain. Look for funding through PTA, grants, and local businesses. Books can also be collected through school book drives, paperbacks withdrawn from the previous year's reading programs, book fairs, book club order points donated by faculty, secondhand stores, public library sales, and donations from local bookstores. Once the SSR Lending Library is established, it takes basic upkeep to maintain: adding new books, discarding damaged and aged books. Annually, promote to faculty the SSR Lending Library through one-on-one conversations, staff meetings, and the staff newsletter. Host the occasional book swap/exchange (see below) to get the books redistributed and remixed.

It's important to remember that the SSR Lending Library is a no fault zone, where the library media specialist and classroom teacher should not get upset or concerned by books that disappear. Consider every lost book a loving home found and a lifelong reader created, or in the making. Any time a classroom teacher sees the classroom bookshelf dwindling, she just has to drop by the SSR Lending Library for a refill.

Book Drive

Host a schoolwide book drive. Coordinate with a local organization (children's hospital, women's shelter) to accept half of the donated books for their guests. Discuss the idea with the parent-teacher organization (PTA/PTO) and student organizations your school has that are involved in community service projects. Students are vital assets to the promotion, planning, and implementation of the project. Advertise in the student newsletter, student newspaper, and school announcement systems before, during, and after. Encourage all students to get involved. Run the book drive. Collect books for all ages. At the conclusion of the drive, keep a portion of the books to add to supplement the SSR Lending Library. The school donates the rest to the local organization.

SSR Book Swap/Exchange

Every classroom should have a bookshelf full of books, but no matter how good the collection on that classroom bookshelf, the students get "bored" seeing the same books on the shelf every day. A way to remix the books to make them look fresh and new without having to spend any money is to host an SSR book swap party after or before school. Invite all faculty to the library media center for an SSR Book Swap once a semester. Consider providing snacks and drinks for the event. In preparation, bring out materials from the SSR Lending Library and display on tables. Attendees bring books from their classroom bookshelves and exchange the books their kids are tired of seeing for a fresh variety of books the library media specialist has displayed on tables and from books others brought to exchange.

Student Book Exchange Days

Get students involved in the fun. Host reading celebrations for students in the library media center. Multiple classes come to the library media center at the same time to talk books and trade books. Invite students to bring a book from home they've already read, enjoyed, and are ready to trade to another student for a different book.

READING PROMOTION

An integral piece to building a reading culture in the school is promoting readership in a visual, informational, and entertaining manner.

Booktalks

Booktalking is an art form that is the regular practice of every library media specialist. Booktalks are scheduled formally with classes. They are also provided informally to individuals and small groups receiving assistance locating reading material in the library media center. When trying to decide which books to promote to classes, choose material found on recommended or award lists, or material written by prolific writers, or material that you or others you respect have read and enjoyed. Consider the books you have many copies of, like those used in reading programs your school participates in annually. For example, in my school I enjoy booktalking books related to an upcoming author visit and the current year's Young Hoosier Book Award program nominees. I know that we have many copies of these books, they are recent publications with a variety of themes and genres, and they are strongly supported by classroom teachers. A great place to find a resource list of books, articles, and Web sites is the American Library Association's Young Adult Library Services Association's "Booktalking" Web site at http://www.ala.org/ala/yalsa/profdev/booktalking.htm.

Get students involved in the action as well. Collaborate with classroom teachers to co-teach a unit on booktalking. Use the best student-created booktalks during televised or audio announcements. I have found that students like having a booktalk they wrote considered for announcements, but do not like having their face on the TV, so we focus the camera on a close-up of the book cover while the student narrates the booktalk in the background.

Bookmarks

School-made bookmarks are an inexpensive way to promote your own school's resources and current reading trends. Decorate one side of the bookmark with student artwork, school logo, themes, or genres. Use the other side of the bookmark to promote available resources of a particular genre, theme, or reading program. Create the list, enlist a teacher or department to generate a favored topic and list, or work with a particular class or team to develop a topic and list.

Posters and Signs

The computer has made life so much easier, take advantage of it. Use your computer to create colorful signs and posters promoting reading. In the corner, include the library logo or school mascot to give the material a personal touch. Display them on walls, endcaps, counters, tops of bookshelves, table centerpieces, and nested in empty shelves. These can also easily be taken down and moved around or replaced with other home-made signs and posters so that patrons don't grow numb to their environment, but instead walk in to little changes and touches of freshness that spark interest. Remember to enlist students to help.

Book Displays

Find ways and places to display reading material in the library media center and other locations throughout the building. Don't do it alone: get teams, classes, and departments to sponsor displays throughout the year. Getting others involved helps engender enthusiasm and interest. Students and teachers see others showing interest in their display. Students and teachers are always interested in knowing how others decorate and display.

Book Club

Host student book clubs before school, during lunch, or after school. These meetings can be as formal or informal as the library media specialist is comfortable with hosting.

Students can be encouraged to read the exact same material, something from the same theme or genre, or a free-for-all anything that meant something to the students. Activities can include directed discussion and informal booktalking or games that encourage book discussion, which can be homemade or commercially purchased. Be creative and use an idea of your own, like Robyn Young, library media specialist at Avon High School, who puts discussion starters on popsicle sticks that students take turns drawing out of a container every time the reading conversation begins to slow down or slide to other topics.

Student Authoring

Use the student newsletter, signs, posters, student announcements, and classroom teachers to help promote a student authoring contest. Accept any original students' work: drawings, poetry, short stories, essays, etc. Gather together a committee of volunteers to review the entries. Select all the entries that meet your criteria; instead of a set number of winners, accept all that meet the criteria. Take those entries and create a "book" published in-house. Make copies for the library media center and classroom bookshelf shelves.

Read-Aloud

Invite administrators and other school personnel to animatedly read aloud for holidays, national and local reading programs/events, and major school events, such as an international festival, science fair, or dance.

Arrange for students to read aloud to special needs classes and local elementary schools. Take this opportunity to collaborate with a classroom teacher on a picture book writing project. It is very rewarding to work with a group of students developing their oral interpretation of literature skills, and then taking them to visit and read to younger students. The hero worship seen on the younger children's faces and the growing feelings of self-worth on the older students' faces cannot be manufactured or replicated in any other way.

Author Visit

An effective author visit causes a drastic, positive change toward building a climate of readers in a school. It effectively impacts students, staff, and parents. The excitement it engenders in all involved is difficult to duplicate through other means. Brenda Crauder, a middle school assistant principal, explains: "A guest author provides an opportunity for students to connect print with people. Seldom do students have the privilege to make a personal connection with an author to solidify the power and importance of the writing process. This experience spawns a new relationship between the reader and books. The result is a greater understanding of the importance reading has on our lives."

Author visits take effort and require advanced planning, so pool together resources with neighboring libraries or schools to share expenses, resources, and responsibilities. We partner with a group of schools in our area, through the leadership of Lu Dayment at Greenwood Middle School. Through her direction and guidance, three to five area schools and at least one public library participate in a community-wide event that generates enough interest to receive notice annually in local papers.

At my school we are able to fund an author visit and reading materials through the generosity of our parent-teacher organization and the commitment of an administration that sees and hears the difference an author visit makes. Through this generous funding, all students are expected to read or be read to at least one book by the author. All staff, not just reading teachers, is encouraged to participate as well. When the author arrives, we reward students by prizing away the books used by classes to prepare for the author visit. Then the author spends hours autographing hundreds of books for our students. A recent author visit was so successful that we had to quickly invest in more copies of the author's books in the library media center to keep up with the demand.

CREATING A COMMUNITY OF FAMILY READERS

Building a community of readers includes helping students and parents develop reading opportunities and habits at home. The library media specialist does anything humanly possible to help families encourage home reading experiences.

Family Reading Together

A child is never too old and it's never too late to start reading aloud as a family. It doesn't necessarily need to be a complete book or article, maybe even just a section or passage that a family member found most interesting or entertaining. Show parents how reading aloud is more than books. It can be song lyrics, student newsletter, mail, menu, nutrition label, Web page, directions, yearbook, newspaper article, game instructions, and so on. To this day I can still remember the warm feeling brought about by moments of being read to by my parents. Just thinking about it even now elicits smells and images of the high ceiling family room of my youth as my father spoke in his deep timbre from a book about warm fuzzies and cold pricklies. And when I bring this memory to my dad, he looks at me with a small smile that seems to warm his face as his eyes begin to sparkle. It's important that parents of today's busy, hectic world understand, as my parents did, the need for these quiet times of oneness with children. The Indiana Library Federation—Association for Indiana Media Educators annually reports a list of Read Aloud Books Too Good to Miss; see http://www.ilfonline.org/AIME/ReadAloud/ReadAloud.htm.

Home Bookshelf

Reward students with books. Instead of rewarding students with candy, food, toys, and other junk, work to change the school philosophy to change the reward to a self-selected book. Reward students for getting caught being good citizens throughout the school, including good behavior and good school practices. Reward students for meeting individual or school reading goals. For example, a school reading goal worth rewarding could be turning in a completed home reading log, completing so many books on the state reading program's list, participating in class content area reading activities, completing all homework for a grading quarter, or meeting a personal, educational, or behavioral goal.

I will not soon forget the first time we rewarded classroom effort and student behavior with books during summer school remediation. Angela Gunkel, seventh grade Language Arts teacher, expressed, "Seeing the faces of my students light up as they selected their free book reward was one of the most touching moments of my teaching career. It was great to hear struggling students say things like, 'This book is mine…I really get to keep it?'"

Public Library

Keep open communication with the public library. The public library should know what's happening in the library media center and the library media center should know what is happening in the public library. Promote public library events and activities to the staff through e-mail and announcements at meetings. Help publicize events to the community through announcements in the student newsletter.

Invite the public library to back-to-school night, new family orientation, or parent-teacher conference events. It has become tradition at my school for our local branch of the public library to set up a table at our new school year student orientation event. They distribute brochures, bookmarks, library give-aways, and have a computer set up to accept new library card registrations. Every year we are all pleased with the number of families that register for a new or replacement public library card at these events.

Newsletter

Stay connected to your students' families by maintaining visibility through the student newsletter. Through the newsletter, reserve a special corner for the library media specialist to promote book reviews, recommended reading lists, the public library connection, home reading habits, and give descriptions on how to access at home the OPAC, online encyclopedia, and other electronic resource subscriptions.

Reading Log

Encourage students and families to maintain a reading log, just as they might have done in elementary school. Help families and students understand how to "snatch" those reading moments and not waste time while waiting for an appointment, traveling as a passenger, waiting for a ride or friend, and other opportunities. Minutes do matter. Even if they are busy and can only grab a few minutes here or there, those minutes add up and make a difference in establishing the practice and habit of reading.

Brochure

Getting information out to parents, students, and staff establishes and grows a reading climate and communication. Brochures take a little time to initially create, but once created, updating them annually is a simple task. Create brochures and display them in strategic locations throughout the building, such as the main office, teacher's lounge, new student registration area, library media center, and sports' entrance. Share brochures at parent and community events. Ideas for brochures include promoting the state reading program for your grade level, orientation to online resources and the school library media center, reading comprehension strategies, family best practices to encourage reading behaviors and skills, and an overview of the school year's reading programs and events.

REFERENCES

American Library Association. "Booktalking." 2006. http://www.ala.org/ala/yalsa/profdev/booktalking.htm. (Accessed 1 June 2006).

Indiana Library Federation—Association for Indiana Media Educators. "Read Aloud Books Too Good to Miss." http://www.ilfonline.org/AIME/ReadAloud/ReadAloud.htm. (Accessed 7 July 2006).

McKenzie, Jamie. "Power Reading and the School Library." *Library Media Connection* 23 (5): 14–19 (2005).

Smith, Frank. *Joining the Literacy Club.* Portsmouth, NH: Heinneman, 1988.

5

Student Reading-Writing-Response Journal Prompts

Students respond in writing to a question posted in class prior to reading. Each day students read, then post in their journal the date, title of what they've been reading, page numbers completed (e.g., pages 12–15), copy the posted reading-writing-response prompt, and finally, their actual, personal response to the prompt as they reflect on the day's reading.

In this chapter educators will find a variety of prompts, sorted into three sections: material with a plot, or informational text, and test readiness terminology. Use these prompts during SSR with Interventions for students' reading-writing-response journal. The prompts are intended to be generic enough to be applicable for most reading, further ensuring student choice in the reading selection process.

Included with each test readiness term are sample prompts using the test language term and easily understood language breakdown and definition.

PROMPTS FOR MATERIAL WITH A PLOT

A

- A problem I have when reading is . . .

- After reading, I wonder . . .

- Analyze how your feelings change as you read this story.

- Analyze the author's ability to write. What does the author do most effectively? What does the author do least effectively?

- Analyze what motivates the main character's behavior.

- Analyze why your feelings change as you read.

- Analyze your emotions as you read. How is the author able to invoke your emotions?

- Are the characters realistic (do they seem like they could be real people)? Why or why not?

- As your reading has progressed, how have the character's feelings changed? Why?

B

- Based on what you've read so far, how do you think the story will end?

- Based on what you've read so far, how does the story make you feel?

- Build a map of the place described in your reading.

C

- Choose a new title for what you are reading. Defend your reasons for the new title.

- Classify the genre of this reading. Defend your answer with example characteristics of the genre, and where you find those characteristics in your reading.

- Classify the antagonists. List the characteristics and events that lead you to that conclusion.

- Classify the protagonists. List the characteristics and events that lead you to that conclusion.

- Compare the plot of what you are reading with your favorite book.

- Compare what is happening to a character in the book with your own or a friend's life.

- Compare where you live to the setting described in what you are reading.

- Contrast the theme of what you are reading with something you read last month.

- Create a comic strip detailing today's reading.

- Create a plot diagram.

From *SSR with Intervention: A School Library Action Research Project* by Leslie B. Preddy. Westport, CT: Libraries Unlimited. Copyright © 2007.

- Create a timeline of events from what you have read so far.

- Create a "WANTED" poster for the antagonist.

- Create an advertisement flyer for the setting as if it were a tourist destination.

- Create an award certificate that you would give to one of the characters. Who would you give it to and why?

D

- Define what is needed to make a good setting.

- Define what is needed for a reader to be able to relate to a character.

- Define what makes an interesting story or poem.

- Describe a character that you would like to meet (which doesn't mean that you think you would like the character, but that you think the character would be interesting). List four questions you would ask.

- Describe experiences or feelings you have had that are similar to the story.

- Describe something you read previously that is similar to this.

- Describe the important ideas in the story.

- Describe the main characters.

- Describe the major conflict. Which side are you on? What would have to happen for you to switch sides?

- Describe the major conflict. Which side are you on? Why?

- Describe the mood of what you are reading.

- Describe the most important event. Give at least three reasons why you think it is the most important event.

- Describe the setting.

- Describe the setting—when and where what you are reading takes place.

- Describe the setting's time and place. Create a new setting that you think would be better for the story. Describe it.

- Describe the setting's time and place. Draw it.

- Describe the setting's time and place. List the clues that helped you identify the setting.

- Describe the similarities and differences between the main character and you.

- Describe the theme (central meaning/message) of your reading.

- Describe what was either believable or unbelievable about your reading. Defend your opinion.

- Describe why you would or would not want to live in the setting.

- Describe your least favorite character and explain why.

- Describe your most favorite character and explain why.

- Differentiate between a good story or poem and a bad story or poem.

- Differentiate between the main character and your favorite teacher.

- Differentiate between the setting of what you are reading and where you live.

- Discuss what images appear in your mind as you read and how the author helped create those images.

- Discuss why you like or dislike what you are reading.

- Do any of the characters' feelings change as you've read? Explain why or why not.

- Do you like what you're reading? Why or why not?

- Does the title fit the story? Why or why not?

- Draw a comic strip for what you just read.

- Draw a graphic novel page for what you just read.

- Draw a line down the center of your paper. On the left, list what you like about what you've read and why. On the right, list what you didn't like and why.

- Draw a line down the center of your paper. On the left, write what you know to be true from what you've read so far. On the right, write your personal opinions about what you've read.

- Draw a line down the center of your paper. Write a cause (why did it happen?) on the left and its effect (what happened?) on the right. Fill in the columns with at least three causes and three effects.

- Draw a map of the setting.

- Draw a picture for what you just read.

- Draw a picture to represent what you just read. Include a sentence explaining what your images mean.

- Draw a Venn diagram. The left circle is for the protagonist. The right circle is for the antagonist. List the characters' traits in their respective circle. Where the two circles join, list the traits they have in common.

- Draw a wanted poster for the antagonist. Be sure to include a picture of the antagonist's face, a list of the antagonist's "crimes" from the story, and the "reward" amount.

- Draw an interpretation of the passage—it may be a picture, symbols, or graphic organizer.

- Draw four objects that represent your reading. Write a sentence for each, telling what each item says about what you've been reading.

From *SSR with Intervention: A School Library Action Research Project* by Leslie B. Preddy. Westport, CT: Libraries Unlimited. Copyright © 2007.

E

- Evaluate the main character's motives.

- Evaluate the quality of the writing. What are good writing traits for this genre?

- Evaluate whether the main character would be worthy of your friendship.

- Evaluate whether the title fits the story.

- Examine a character's motivation.

- Explain how you have been surprised by what you are reading.

- Explain the process you go through when choosing something to read for pleasure.

- Explain what kind of reader would like this book most.

- Explain why somebody should or should not read this book.

F

- Formulate your own conclusion for what you are reading.

- Formulate your own opinions about why your favorite character is necessary to the story.

- Formulate your own opinions about why your least favorite character is necessary to the story.

- From what you read, choose an event that you can connect to a world event. Describe the book's event and how it connects to a world event.

- From what you read, choose an event that you can connect to another book. Describe the event and how it connects to the other book.

- From what you read, choose an event that you can connect to your life. Describe the event and how it connects to your life.

G

- Give an example of when a character had an important choice to make. What did the character do? What other choices did the character have?

- Give an example of when a character had an important choice to make. What would you have done differently?

- Give an example of when a character had an important choice to make. What would you have done similar? Why?

H

- How are the characters similar to real people in your life?

- How are the characters similar to those in other stories?

- How are the problems in this story similar to problems you have experienced in your life?

- How did the reading make you feel? Why?

- How do the characters deal with the challenges and problems they face?

- How do the characters feel about one another? Defend your reasoning with specific examples from the story.

- How does the author characterize the characters (dialogue, direct commentary, actions)? Explain.

- How does the setting affect the characters?

- How does the setting affect the plot?

- How does what you are reading contrast with a novel you were recently assigned to read in school?

- How does what you've been reading remind you of your life?

- How have your feelings about this book changed as you've been reading?

- How is the author able to make the characters believable to you?

- How is the setting important to the story?

- How is the setting similar to places you have been or seen in your life?

- How is the setting similar to the setting in other stories you've read?

- How is this different from other things you've read?

- How is this similar to other things you've read?

- How would changing the setting's place change the story?

- How would changing the setting's time change the story?

- How would this story be changed if you were in it?

- How would this story compare to real life?

- How would you explain the plot of this story to somebody interested in reading it?

- How would you respond to what you just read if you were in this story?

I

- I believe . . .

- I chose this to read because . . .

- I didn't get it when . . .

- I enjoy reading when . . .

- I feel like reading when . . .

- I like to read . . .

- I like to read about . . .

- I predict . . .

- I think . . .

- I think I would be a better reader if . . .

- I think the outcome will be . . .

- I think this is similar to . . . because . . .

- I was surprised when . . .

- I wonder . . .

- I would rather read than . . .

- I would read more if . . .

- Identify the main characters. Describe what has happened that makes you believe they are the main characters.

- Identify the protagonist. Identify the antagonist. Describe what has happened that makes you believe they are the main characters.

- Identify what the author has done to try to keep you reading the book.

- If I were asked if I'm a good reader, I would say . . .

- If I were this author, I would have written . . .

- If the author were here, what would you say and ask him or her?

- If this story were real, describe where in the real world it would take place.

- If this story were real, the world would be different because . . .

- If you could add a character to the story, who would you add and what would you have that character do?

- If you could add a magic object to what you are reading, what would it be and how would you have it used in the story?

- If you could change the title, what would you change it to and why?

- If you could change what you're reading, how would you change it?

- If you could talk to the author, what questions would you ask? Why?

- If you could talk to the author, what would you want to tell the author about yourself? Why? How does that relate to what you've been reading?

- If you were a character in this book, who would you be? Why?

- If you were the author, how would this end?

- If you were the author, what would you change? Why?

- If you were the author, what would you have happening next?

- If you were to pick five items to represent this story, what would they be and why?

- In a few paragraphs, summarize what you read *today.*

- In a few sentences, summarize what you read *today.*

- Infer events in the character's past to make him or her react as he or she is now.

- In four to six sentences, describe several insights you've gained from your reading.

- Is the setting described well enough to put a picture of it in your mind? Why or why not?

- Is this reading a good choice for you? How did you come to that decision?

- Is what you are reading believable? Why or why not?

J

- Justify how one of the characters is like you and how the character is different from you.

- Justify how realistic or unrealistic the setting is to you.

- Justify the antagonist's behavior.

- Justify the protagonist's behavior.

K

- Keeping what you've already read in mind, how do you think it should end?

- Knock on the door of your favorite character. What would you say?

- Knock on the door of your least favorite character. What would you say?

L

- List all the words that come to mind when thinking of what you just read.

- List at least three problems the characters faced. Which was the most life-changing? Explain.

- List five characters as well as their personality and physical traits.

- List five events in order of importance (*not* in order of occurrence).

- List five major events in order from which happened first to last.

- List the events, in order, that have happened so far in what you've been reading.

- List the personality characteristics of the main character (feelings, interests, behaviors, etc.).

- List the physical characteristics of the main character (clothing, physical features, etc.).

- List the reasons why another person should or should not read this.

- List three difficult words from your reading. Based on context clues, what do you think those words mean? How important are they to understanding the story?

- List three events from your story that could happen in real life. Defend your answer.

- List three events from your story that could NOT happen in real life. Defend your answer.

- List three new vocabulary words from your reading. What can you tell about them from their structure? What can you tell about them from their context?

- List three questions you have about what you've read.

M

- Make a map of the setting. Label important places.

- Make a timeline of the events that have occurred in your book so far.

- My life connects to the reading in this way . . .

N

- Name a character whose opinion or feelings have changed. How have they changed? What caused the character's opinion or feelings to change?

- Name the character most like you. What makes this character so similar to you?

- Name the most important character. What makes this character so important in the story?

- Name the most interesting character. What makes this character so interesting?

- Name the most powerful character. What makes this character powerful to the story?

- Number your paper one to ten. List the top ten reasons you like what you have been reading.

O

- One reason this is worth reading . . .

- Organize your thoughts. What makes a story readable?

- Outline the important events of what you are reading.

- Outline the plot.

P

- Pick out two to four words from what you are reading that you had difficulty understanding. Interpret what you *think* each word means based on context clues (other words around that word that might help you interpret what the author means).

- Pick the phrase from what you are reading that made you think. Interpret what the author meant.

- Plan a trip you would take with one of the characters. Who would you pick and why? Where would you go and why? What would you do and why?

From *SSR with Intervention: A School Library Action Research Project* by Leslie B. Preddy. Westport, CT: Libraries Unlimited. Copyright © 2007.

- Predict the main character's reaction to what you think will happen next.

- Predict the story's ending.

- Predict what the antagonist will do next.

- Predict what the protagonist will do next.

- Predict what will happen next.

- Pretend what you are reading is nominated for a national award. Explain why you think it should or should not receive an award.

- Pretend you are a character in the story having a flashback. Describe what is happening.

- Pretend you are a famous reporter on TV. Write a story for the evening news about what you read.

- Pretend you are a talk show host and two characters are the guests on your show. Which characters would you choose and why? List two questions that you, the host, would ask each character.

- Pretend you are the friend of one of the characters. Write the character a letter.

- Pretend you get to create the music soundtrack for what you've been reading. What five songs would you include? Write an explanation for each song: why would you include it, how does the song connect to events?

- Pretend you have special powers and could put yourself in your reading. Where would you put yourself and why? How would you being there change the story?

- Pretend your job is to write magazine ads. Create an ad for what you've been reading.

- Prove how reading this can change or impact the reader's life.

- Prove the theme of what you are reading (bravery, loyalty, friendship, loneliness, etc.).

- Prove what the author is trying to tell you about life (the moral).

Q

- Question the main character's motivation.

- Quote a passage and respond to it. How does that passage make you feel?

R

- Record how your reading made you feel.

- Record the questions you have about your reading.

- Relate what you have been reading to events in your life or around the world.

- Represent the reading with an illustration.

- Represent the reading with art.

From *SSR with Intervention: A School Library Action Research Project* by Leslie B. Preddy. Westport, CT: Libraries Unlimited. Copyright © 2007.

S

- Select a quote from your reading that you liked. What made you pick it? How does it make you pause and think?

- Summarize what has happened so far.

- Summarize what you just read. Make me want to read it!

- Summarize what you read today.

- Summarize your favorite book. Make me want to read it!

- Support the author's choice of setting (time and place).

- Support the main character's reasons for his or her behavior.

T

- Tell me about the main character. What kind of person is he or she?

- The antagonist reminds me of . . .

- The best part of this reading was when . . .

- The protagonist reminds me of . . .

- The things I thought about as I read are . . .

- Think of a problem that a character had to face. Write the problem and how the character solved it or is working to solve it. If you were that character, what would you do differently?

- Thinking about what you just read, draw the picture that appears in your mind.

- This connects to my life . . .

- This part of my reading is important because . . .

- This plot reminds me of another plot . . .

- This reading reminds me of another reading . . .

- This reminds me of . . .

- This setting reminds me of . . .

- This text relates to my life because . . .

- This theme reminds me of . . .

- Trace the history of the main character.

- Trace the main character's motivation.

- Trace the story's timeline.

U

- Use a graphic organizer to represent what you have read so far.

- Use a web to graphically organize what you have read so far.

- Use pictures to represent what you have read so far.

- Using outline form, describe what is needed for a poem to be effective.

- Using outline form, describe what is needed for a story to be effective.

- Usually a reader imagines the places being described in the story. Draw a picture of the image you have in your mind from this story. What do you usually see in your mind when reading a story?

- Usually an author uses descriptive words to allow us to see the setting. How does this author do that? What words do you usually use?

- Usually an author uses descriptive words to set the mood. How does this author do this? What words do you usually use?

V

- Verbalize (on paper) what a character has been thinking, but hasn't said out loud. Explain.

- Visualize the setting. Draw it. Include a key.

W

- What are some things you do when you don't understand what you're reading?

- What are the important events? Why do you think they are important?

- What are the two most important ideas from what you've been reading?

- What are two emotions the main character has felt? What made the main character feel that way?

- What book does this story remind you of and why?

- What character is like you? Describe how he or she is like you?

- What did the author do to try to keep you interested? Why did the author succeed or fail?

- What do you find difficult about reading this?

- What do you like about what you are reading?

- What do you see in your mind when reading the story?

- What do you think will happen next?

- What do you want to happen next?

- What do you want to read next? Why?

From *SSR with Intervention: A School Library Action Research Project* by Leslie B. Preddy. Westport, CT: Libraries Unlimited. Copyright © 2007.

- What does the author do that causes you to want to read more?

- What does this book remind you of?

- What does this story teach you about life?

- What emotions do you feel about your reading? Describe what is going on in the reading that makes you feel that way.

- What emotions did you feel while you read? Give details from your reading that made you feel that way.

- What event could have happened in real life? What would be similar in real life? What would be different in real life?

- What fix-up strategies did you use when you didn't understand what you were reading?

- What fix-up strategies were helpful for making sense of the reading?

- What has been the most important part of what you've been reading?

- What has been the most interesting part of your reading?

- What has happened so far? What do you think will happen next?

- What have the characters taught you about life?

- What have you been reading? What does it remind you of in your own life?

- What have you found boring about what you've been reading? What made it boring? If you were the author, what would you do to make it more interesting?

- What have you learned about life from the characters?

- What have you learned about life from this story?

- What have you learned about life from what you're reading?

- What I know so far . . .

- What I've learned about life from these characters is . . .

- What I've learned about life from the story is . . .

- What I've learned so far . . .

- What ideas do you have about what is going to happen? What clues have you read to give you those ideas?

- What if . . .

- What is something you've learned from your reading?

- What is the author trying to tell you about life? Defend this moral.

- What is the best book you've ever read? What made it so good?

- What is the funniest part of what you've been reading? Explain.

- What is the genre? What clues make you believe that?

- What is the happiest part of what you've been reading? Explain.

- What is the main idea? Defend your answer.

- What is the mood of what you're reading (happy, sad, funny, serious, etc.)? Defend your idea.

- What is the most believable part of what you've been reading? Explain.

- What is the most serious part of what you've been reading? Explain.

- What is the most unbelievable part of what you've been reading? Explain.

- What is the saddest part of what you've been reading? Explain.

- What is the theme of what you are reading? What clues make you believe that?

- What is the title of what you are reading? How does it fit the story? If you don't know yet how it fits the story, what is your best guess?

- What is your favorite part of the book you're reading? Why?

- What lessons does this teach you about life?

- What message or lesson was conveyed?

- What moral, or life-lesson, can be found in what you are reading? Discuss what you think.

- What object is important to the story? Draw it. Write an explanation for why you feel it is important.

- What passage describes how you want to live your life? Why?

- What problem is currently being faced? Write what you think would be the best way to solve the problem.

- What problem faced by a character was the most life-changing? Explain.

- What problems have you encountered as you read? What fix-up strategies helped?

- What problems have you encountered as you read? What problems did you not have strategies for and could use some help with?

- What questions do you have that haven't been answered? How do you think they'll be resolved?

- What questions would you like answered about your reading? Would you like the reading better if you knew those answers now? Why?

- What skills do you need to be a good reader?

- What special way did the author write (for example, flashbacks, told in first person, multiple voice narrative, foreshadowing, descriptive words that create visual images in your mind, etc.)? Did that make reading it better or worse? Explain.

- What surprises you in this story? Explain why.

- What this has taught me about myself is . . .

- What was going through your mind as you read?

- What words does the author use to help create a picture in your mind?

- What words does the author use to help you build feelings about the characters?

- What would be a good contrast to the setting of what you are reading?

- What would you infer about the author's motives for writing this?

- What you are reading is going to be made into a movie. Create the movie poster.

- What you are reading is going to be made into a movie. List the songs you would include in the soundtrack and why.

- What you are reading is going to be made into a movie. Make a list of five characters, what famous actor will play each character, and what about the character makes that actor the best choice for the part.

- What you are reading is going to be made into a movie. You are the movie executive who chooses the location for the filming. Where would you choose and why?

- When I am trying to read, I get angry when . . .

- Which character do you like best? Why?

- Which character do you like least? Why?

- Who are the characters? Describe who they are, what they look like, and how they are connected.

- Who is the author? What do you know about the author? What do you imagine the author must be like?

- Who is the most important character to you? Why?

- Who is the most interesting character in the book and why?

- Who tells the story? How do you know?

- Who tells the story? How would the story be different if a different character told the story instead?

- Why did you choose this to read? Give at least three reasons.

- Why do you think the author chose this title?

- Why do you think the author wrote this?

- Without using complete sentences or paragraphs, reflect on today's reading.

- Would you be friends with the antagonist? Why or why not? Support with evidence from your reading.

- Would you be friends with the main character? Why or why not? Support with evidence from your life.

- Would you read other books by this author? Why or why not?

- Would you recommend this book to friends? Why or why not?

- Write a booktalk persuading another person to read this without giving too much away.

- Write a detailed summary of what you just read.

- Write a journal entry as if you were a certain character from your reading.

- Write a letter to the author discussing and questioning what you've read.

- Write a newspaper article about what you are reading.

- Write a paragraph describing the setting.

- Write a quote from what you are reading that has meaning for you. Explain why you chose this quote.

- Write a quote from your reading that connects to your life. What did it mean to what you've been reading? What did it mean to your life?

- Write a review of what you just read (summary plus personal opinions).

- Write a summary of what you've read so far.

- Write about a situation a character experiences. Write about a similar situation you experienced.

- Write about how one character feels. Write about a time you felt that way too.

- Write an editorial, an opinion essay, about an event from your reading.

- Write an e-mail to a character.

- Write an e-mail to your best friend, pretending that you live in the setting from your reading.

- Write an obituary for the antagonist.

- Write an obituary for the protagonist.

- Write down one word from your reading that you didn't know. What is your guess about what it means? How did you make that guess?

- Write the biography for one character.

- Write the cause and effect of four events.

- Write the names of all the characters all over your paper. Use arrows to connect characters who know each other. Write on the line of the arrow their relationship (for example: Mom, best friend, school bully, etc.).

Y

- You are a talk show host and will be interviewing one of the characters. Who would you interview and why? List the five questions you believe are most important, but haven't been answered by your readings.

- You are being sent to live in what you are reading. List the five things you would bring with you and why those items would be helpful and important.

From *SSR with Intervention: A School Library Action Research Project* by Leslie B. Preddy. Westport, CT: Libraries Unlimited. Copyright © 2007.

PROMPTS FOR INFORMATIONAL TEXT

A

- After reading and learning, what do you want to know more about?

B

- Before reading, what did you think you already knew? Where were you right? Where were you wrong?

C

- Conflicting information can be confusing. How did what you read conflict with other opinions or ideas?
- Connect what you read to world events.

D

- Do you believe the author to be telling the truth? Defend your reasons.
- Draw a line down the center of your paper. On the left, write facts from what you've read. On the right, write your personal opinions about what you've read.
- Draw a Venn diagram. Before you read, write in the left circle what you think you already know about the topic. After you read, write in the right circle what you learned about topic that you didn't know before. Where the circles connect, write what you thought to be true that the author confirmed with what you read.

E

- Envision the author standing before you. What would you say to him or her?
- Explain, in your own words, what you just read.

F

- For better understanding, I need more information on . . .
- Formulate your own conclusion to what you are reading.
- From this reading I learned . . .

G

- Great ideas can come from your reading. What ideas did your reading give you?

From *SSR with Intervention: A School Library Action Research Project* by Leslie B. Preddy. Westport, CT: Libraries Unlimited. Copyright © 2007.

H

- How can you tell the difference between fact and the author's opinions?

- How does what you read compare to other things you've read on this topic?

- How does what you read relate to the world?

- How does what you read relate to your community?

- How does what you read relate to your life?

- How does your understanding of the topic change after reading this?

I

- I can relate this to my life . . .

- I liked the idea of . . .

- I noticed . . .

- I was surprised . . .

- I wonder . . .

- In a few paragraphs, summarize what you read today.

- In four to six sentences, describe several insights you've gained from your reading.

- Is it fact or opinion? Defend your reasoning.

- Is the author being fair or biased? Defend your answer.

- Is the information up-to-date? Does it need to be? Defend your answer.

J

- Jump to conclusions. Explain why you think you were asked to read this.

- Justify why you think you were asked to read this material.

L

- List some important words the author used and what you think each word means.

- List the important facts from your reading.

- List what you learned from your reading.

M

- Make an outline based on what you just read.

- My opinion on this topic has been changed by . . .

N

- Name the five most important facts?
- Name the five most interesting facts?

O

- Organize your thoughts. List the important facts in order of importance.

P

- Pretend you disagree with what you read. Write a letter to the editor complaining about what you just read.
- Pretend you have to defend what you read to a critic of the subject. What would you say?
- Pretend your job is to write magazine ads. Create an ad for what you've been reading.

Q

- Question the author's motives. What was the author's purpose (inform, persuade, teach, etc.) for writing this. Defend your answer.

R

- Record the author's purpose (inform, persuade, teach, etc.). What do you find in the writing, including the language, format or organization the author uses, to make you believe this way?
- Record how your reading made you feel.
- Record the questions you have about your reading.
- Retell what you just read.

S

- State the important points to what you just read.
- Summarize what you just read.
- Summarize what you read today.

T

- Things I thought about as I read are . . .
- This connects to my life . . .
- This reading is important because . . .

- This reading is interesting because . . .

- This reminds me of . . .

- This text relates to my life because . . .

U

- Underline key words in a summary you write about the reading.

- Using outline form, describe what is needed for informational text to be effective.

V

- Visualize what you read. Draw what you are visualizing.

W

- What are some things you do when you don't understand what you're reading?

- What are the most important ideas the author expresses?

- What are the two most important ideas from what you've been reading? Why do you think they are important?

- What did you already know about this topic? What did you learn?

- What did you believe before you read? What beliefs have changed after you read?

- What did you learn about this topic?

- What did you like about how the author organized information? Why

- What do you find difficult about reading this?

- What does this teach you?

- What experiences have you had in your life that helped you understand what you read?

- What fix-up strategies did you use when you didn't understand what you were reading?

- What fix-up strategies were helpful for making sense of the reading?

- What has the author done to try to make this interesting?

- What is the main idea? Explain.

- What I've learned so far . . .

- What problems have you encountered as you read? What fix-up strategies helped?

- What problems have you encountered as you read? What problems did you not have strategies for and could use some help with?

- What questions do you have about the information that weren't answered? How do you think those questions can be resolved?

- What questions do you now have about this topic?

- What questions would you like answered about your reading? Would you like the reading better if it had answered those questions? Why?

- What research does the author use to defend his or her point? How do you decide whether the research is valid or not?

- What was easy about what you read? What was hard?

- What will you do with this information?

- What would you infer about the author's motives for writing this? Defend your answer with examples from the text.

- Why do you think the author chose this title? How does it fit with what you read?

- Write a letter to the author discussing and questioning what you read.

- Write a newspaper article about what you read.

- Write a summary as if it were a special news report on TV. "We interrupt your regularly scheduled program for this important message . . . "

- Write an editorial about what you read.

- Write an e-mail to the author. Give your informed opinion about what the author wrote.

- Write down one word from your reading that you didn't know. What is your guess about what it means? How did you make that guess?

- Write the main idea of what you are reading. What are your reasons for thinking it is the main idea?

Y

- You are the illustrator. Draw images of the important facts. Give your drawings captions.

PROMPTS AND TEST READINESS TERMS

Analyze

Break apart—
Study each piece closely.
Tell about all of the parts.

When *analyzing* look closely at all the parts or
ideas to best explain how they are related.

Sample prompts:

Analyze how your feelings change as you read this story and why.

Analyze the author's ability to write. What does the author do most effectively? What does the
author do least effectively?

Analyze what motivates the main character's behavior.

Analyze why your feelings change as you read.

Analyze your emotions as you read. How is the author able to invoke your emotions?

Classify

Sort—
Arrange into categories by type.

When *classifying,* look closely at the subject matter
to put in groups that are alike.

Sample prompts:

Classify the antagonists. List the characteristics and events that lead you to that conclusion.

Classify the genre of this reading. Defend your answer with example characteristics of the genre, and where you find those characteristics in your reading.

Classify the protagonists. List the characteristics and events that lead you to that conclusion.

Compare

Alike—
What do they share to make them alike?
Tell all the ways they are alike.

When *comparing* things, look closely to find all things
that are alike between them.

Sample prompts:

Compare the plot of what you are reading with your favorite book.

Compare what is happening to a character in the book with your own or a friend's life.

Compare where you live to the setting described in what you are reading.

How does what you just read compare to other things you've read?

How would this story compare to real life?

Contrast

Different—
What is the difference?
Opposite of similar—Tell all the ways they are different.

When *contrasting* things, look closely to
find all things that are different between them.

Sample prompts:

Contrast the theme of what you are reading with something you read last month.

How does what you are reading contrast with a novel you were assigned to read in school and didn't like reading?

What would be a good contrast to the setting of what you are reading?

Create

Build—
Form an idea or product.

When *creating*, you produce something
through imagination or skill.

Sample prompts:

Create a comic strip detailing today's reading.

Create a plot diagram.

Create a timeline of events from what you have read so far.

Create an advertisement flyer for the setting as if it were a tourist destination.

Describe the setting's time and place. Create a new setting that you think would be better for the story. Describe it.

Pretend you get to create the music soundtrack for what you've been reading. What five songs would you include? Write an explanation for each song: why would you include it, how does the song connect to events?

Pretend your job is to write magazine ads. Create an ad for what you've been reading.

What words does the author use to help create a picture in your mind?

Define

Characterize—
Identify what is important.
A detailed explanation.

When *defining* something, look at it carefully
and identify the qualities that make it meaningful.

Sample prompts:

Define what is needed for a reader to be able to relate to a character.

Define what is needed to make a good setting.

Define what makes an interesting story or poem.

Describe

Tell about—
Tell ALL about.
Make a picture with words.

When *describing* something,
use descriptive words and many details.

Sample prompts:

Describe the major conflict. What side are you on?

Describe the mood of what you are reading.

Describe the setting's time and place. List the clues that helped you identify the setting.

Describe the theme (central meaning/message) of your reading.

Describe your least favorite character and explain why.

Describe your most favorite character and explain why.

From what you've read, choose an event that you can connect to a world event. Describe the book's event and how it connects to a world event.

From what you've read, choose an event that you can connect to your life. Describe the event and how it connects to your life.

Differentiate

Not alike—
Study the differences.
Show how to tell them apart.

When you *differentiate*,
explain the difference between things.

Sample prompts:

Differentiate between a good story or poem and a bad story or poem.

Differentiate between the main character and your favorite teacher.

Differentiate between the setting of what you are reading and where you live.

How is this different from other things you've read?

If this story were real, the world would be different because . . .

What event could have happened in real life? What would be similar in real life? What would be different in real life?

Who tells the story? How would it be different if a different character told the story instead?

Discuss

Investigate—
Carefully scrutinize.
Present in detail.

When *discussing* something,
closely examine the subject in detail.

Sample prompts:

Discuss what images appear in your mind as you read and how the author helped create those
images.

Discuss why you like or dislike what you are reading.

What moral—or life-lesson—can be found in what you are reading? Discuss what think.

Write a letter to the author discussing and questioning what you read.

Evaluate

Judge—
Closely examine all parts.
Decide what is good and bad, how do you feel about it?

When *evaluating*, look closely to determine
what is important and significant.

Sample prompts:

Evaluate the main character's motives.

Evaluate the quality of the writing.

Evaluate whether the main character would be worthy of your friendship.

Evaluate whether the title fits the story.

Explain

Give details—
Clarify with simple, clear words.
Put what you know in your own words.

When *explaining* something, give reasons why things happened
or give reasons for how you got your answer.

Sample prompts:

Explain the process you go through when choosing something to read for pleasure.

Explain what kind of reader would like this book most.

How does the author characterize the characters (dialogue, direct commentary, actions, etc.)? Explain.

Pretend what you are reading is nominated for a national award. Explain why you think it should or should not receive an award.

Pretend you get to create the music soundtrack for what you've been reading. What five songs would you include? Write an explanation for each song: why would you include it, how does the song connect to events?

What object is important in the story? Draw it. Write an explanation for why you feel it is important.

Formulate

> Put together—
> Create, devise, make, plan, prepare.
> Put together in your own words.
>
> When *formulating* a response, through study and analysis,
> create personal thoughts, opinions, and ideas.

Sample prompts:

Formulate your own conclusion to what you are reading.

Formulate your own opinions about why your favorite character is necessary to the story.

Formulate your own opinions about why your least favorite character is necessary to the story.

Identify

Find/Locate—
Recognize distinctive characteristics.

When *identifying* something,
look closely and explain what makes it unique.

Sample prompts:

Describe the setting's time and place. List the clues that helped you identify the setting.

Identify the main characters. Describe what has happened that makes you believe they are the main characters.

Identify the protagonist. Identify the antagonist. Describe what has happened that makes you believe they are the main characters.

Identify what the author has done to try to keep you reading the book.

Infer

An educated guess—
Read between the lines.
Understand what is not being said.

When *inferring*, look closely at what words are used and how
to make a best guess about what is meant, but not written.

Sample prompts:

Infer events in the character's past causing him or her react as he or she is now.

What would you infer about the author's motives for writing this?

Interpret

Explain—
Construe meaning.
Give the meaning or significance of it.

When *interpreting* something, think and examine it carefully,
then explain in an easy-to-understand way.

Sample prompts:

Draw an interpretation of the passage—it may be a picture, symbols, or graphic organizer.

Pick out two to four words from what you are reading that you had difficulty understanding. Interpret what you think each word means based on context clues (other words around that word that might help you interpret what the author means).

Pick the phrase from what you are reading that made you think. Interpret what the author meant.

Which characters would you interpret to be bad? What has the author written that leads you to those interpretations?

Which characters would you interpret to be good? What has the author written that leads you to those interpretations?

Justify

Prove—
Show to be right.
Give reason for; substantiate; validate.

To *justify*, give good reasons to defend
a response, reaction, idea, or thought.

Sample prompts:

Justify how one of the characters is like you and how the character is different from you.

Justify how realistic or unrealistic the setting is to you.

Justify the antagonist's behavior.

Justify the protagonist's behavior.

Justify why you think you were asked to read this material.

List

```
Record—
Listing of items.

When creating a list about an event or thing,
provide all of the details or all of the steps in order.
```

Sample prompts:

List five events in order of importance (not in order of occurrence).

List five major events in order from which happened first to last.

List three new vocabulary words from your reading. What can you tell about them from their structure? What can you tell about them from their context?

List three questions you have about what you've read.

Pretend you are a talk show host and two characters are the guests on your show. Which characters would you choose and why? List two questions that you, the host, would ask each character.

What you are reading is going to be made into a movie. List the songs you would include in the soundtrack and why.

You are a talk show host and will be interviewing one of the characters. Who would you interview and why? List the five questions you believe are most important, but haven't been answered by your readings.

You are being sent to live in what you are reading. List the five things you would bring with you and why those items would be helpful and important.

From *SSR with Intervention: A School Library Action Research Project* by Leslie B. Preddy. Westport, CT: Libraries Unlimited. Copyright © 2007.

Main Idea

Major theme—
Carefully analyze.
Find most important idea reader should gain.

When looking at the *main idea*,
look for the most important idea or reason.

Sample prompts:

What is the main idea? Defend your answer.

What is the main idea? Explain.

Write the main idea of what you are reading and what your reasons are for thinking it is the main idea.

Write the main idea for what you are reading. Why do you think it is the main idea?

Outline

> Condense—
> Summary or preliminary account.
>
> When *outlining* something,
> create a brief description or organized listing.

Sample prompts:

Outline the important events of what you are reading.

Outline the plot.

Using outline form, describe what is needed for informational text to be effective.

Using outline form, describe what is needed for a poem to be effective.

Using outline form, describe what is needed for a story to be effective.

From *SSR with Intervention: A School Library Action Research Project* by Leslie B. Preddy. Westport, CT: Libraries Unlimited. Copyright © 2007.

Predict

```
Forecast—
Make a guess as to what to expect next.
Foresee what is coming.

When predicting,
give an educated guess as to what will happen next.
```

Sample prompts:

I predict . . .

Predict the main character's reaction to what you think will happen next.

Predict the story's ending.

Predict what the antagonist will do next.

Predict what the protagonist will do next.

Predict what will happen next.

Prove

Provide evidence—
Examine closely.
Use proof to confirm theory, thought, idea, concept, etc.

To *prove* something, give details and examples
to defend what is thought or believed.

Sample prompts:

Prove how reading this can change or impact the reader's life.

Prove the theme of what you are reading (bravery, loyalty, friendship, loneliness, etc.).

Prove what the author is trying to tell you about life (the moral).

Summarize

Sum it up—
Put it all together.
Retell with just the basic facts, main ideas.

To *summarize*, give a brief description of
what happened with only a few details.

Sample prompts:

In a few paragraphs, summarize what you've read today.

Summarize what you just read. Make me want to read it!

Summarize your favorite book. Make me want to read it!

Write a brief summary of what you've read.

Write a review of what you just read (summary plus personal opinions).

Write a summary as if it were a special news report on TV. "We interrupt your regularly scheduled program for this important message . . . "

Write a summary of what you just read.

Support

> Give the facts—
> Look for details.
> Give the reason, argument, information, facts.
>
> To *support*, examine closely
> to give evidence and reasons.

Sample prompts:

Support the author's choice of setting (time and place).

Support the main character's reasons for his or her behavior.

Would you be friends with the main character? Why or why not? Support with evidence from your own life.

Would you be friends with the main character? Why or why not? Support with evidence from your reading.

From *SSR with Intervention: A School Library Action Research Project* by Leslie B. Preddy. Westport, CT: Libraries Unlimited. Copyright © 2007.

Trace

Find the path—
Outline or list the steps
In order from beginning to end.

When *tracing*, examine thoroughly
and carefully sketch from beginning to end.

Sample prompts:

Trace the history of the main character.

Trace the main character's motivation.

Trace the story's timeline.

Usually

Sample prompts:

Usually a reader imagines the places being described in the story. Draw a picture of the image you have from this story. What do you usually see in your mind when reading a story?

Usually an author uses descriptive words to allow us to set the mood. How does this author do that? What words do you usually use?

Usually an author uses descriptive words to allow us to set the setting. How does this author do that? What words do you usually use?

6

Reproducibles

This chapter is devoted to reproducibles for your school to use with SSR with Interventions. Included are informational bookmarks, home reading log, reading-writing-response journal templates, teacher conference log, and a teacher observation log.

RESOURCES FOR TEACHERS

SSR with Interventions Observation Log

Students	Date:	Date:	Date:	Date:	Date:	Date:	Date:	Date:	Date:	Date:	Date:	Date:	Date:	Date:	Date:	Date:	Date:	Date:
1.																		
2.																		
3.																		
4.																		
5.																		
6.																		
7.																		
8.																		
9.																		
10.																		
11.																		
12.																		
13.																		
14.																		
15.																		
16.																		
17.																		
18.																		
19.																		
20.																		
21.																		
22.																		
23.																		
24.																		
25.																		
26.																		
27.																		
28.																		
29.																		
30.																		
31.																		
32.																		
33.																		
34.																		
35.																		
36.																		
37.																		
38.																		

O = Student On-task (reading)

X = Student Off-task (sleeping, mock reading, need reminding to keep reading)

C = Student-Teacher Reader's Conference (had personal conversation with student)

J = Student's Journal read (personal comment placed in journal)

Conference Log

Student Name: _____

Conference Date: _____

What Student Is Reading Today: _____

Discussion Notes:

Conference Date: _____

What Student Is Reading Today: _____

Discussion Notes:

Conference Date: _____

What Student Is Reading Today: _____

Discussion Notes:

RESOURCES FOR STUDENTS

Home Reading Log

Name: _____ Week of: _____

MONDAY—read for 20 minutes

Title: _____ Page ___ through page ___

Brief Summary, Questions, Comments, or Personal Thoughts: _____

_____

_____

Discuss what I read with a parent. Parent Signature: _____

TUESDAY—read for 20 minutes   Title: _____

Brief Summary, Questions, Comments, or Personal Thoughts: _____

_____

_____

Discuss what I read with a parent. Parent Signature: _____

WEDNESDAY—read for 20 minutes Title: _____

Brief Summary, Questions, Comments, or Personal Thoughts: _____

_____

_____

Discuss what I read with a parent. Parent Signature: _____

THURSDAY—read for 20 minutes   Title: _____

Brief Summary, Questions, Comments, or Personal Thoughts: _____

_____

_____

Discuss what I read with a parent. Parent Signature: _____

BONUS: Read for 20 minutes Friday.   Parent Signature: _____

BONUS: Read for 20 minutes Saturday.   Parent Signature: _____

BONUS: Read for 20 minutes Sunday.   Parent Signature: _____

From *SSR with Intervention: A School Library Action Research Project* by Leslie B. Preddy. Westport, CT: Libraries Unlimited. Copyright © 2007.

Reading-Writing-Response Journal—My Idea Page

Name: _____

Fill in anything you can now, and then continue to add to it as you experience new fiction and informational text.

Authors I like:	Informational text I like:
Series and Titles I like:	Themes and genres I enjoy reading:

Reading-Writing-Response Journal—My Idea Page

Name: _____

Fill in anything you can now, and then continue to add to it as you experience new fiction and informational text.

Authors I like:	Informational text I like:
Series and Titles I like:	Themes and genres I enjoy reading:

Reading-Writing-Response Journal

Name: _____ Date: _____

Title: _____ Page _____ through page _____

Reading-Writing Prompt: _____

_____

My Response: _____

_____

_____

_____

_____

_____

_____

_____

_____

Reading-Writing-Response Journal

Name: _____ Date: _____

Title: _____ Page _____ through page _____

Reading-Writing Prompt: _____

_____

My Response: _____

_____

_____

_____

_____

_____

_____

_____

_____

T-Chart

Topic: _____

Topic: _____

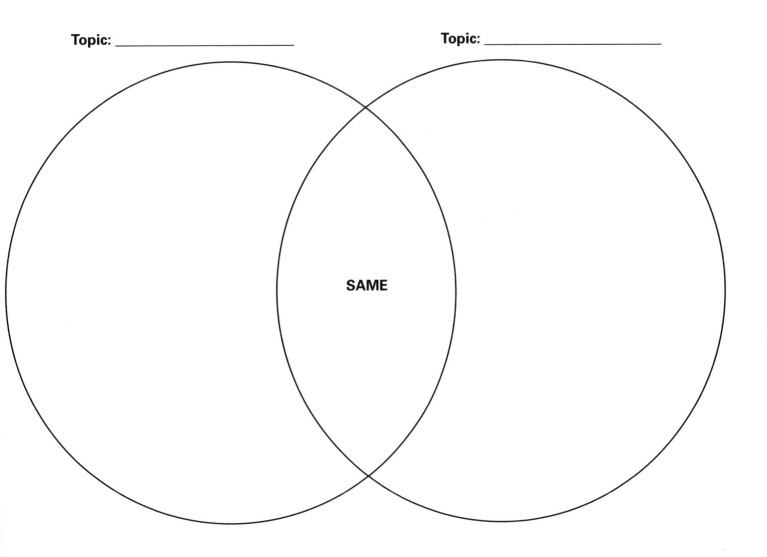

SAME

BOOKMARKS

Parents Take Note

Tips & Tricks to Encourage Reading

Being a successful reader is a predictor for future success as a working adult.

Help your adolescent increase his or her chances of success in high school and beyond by building a family of readers.

How to encourage an adolescent to read:

- Make regular visits to the public library and bookstores/sales.
- Encourage your child to have reading material with him or her wherever he or she goes.
- Read aloud and discuss what you think before, during, and after reading an interesting passage from newspapers, magazines, Web sites, books, and other reading material.
- Help your child build a home library—a bookshelf containing fiction and nonfiction of personal interest.
- Encourage your child to read, or read together, at least 15 minutes every day.
- Allow your child to have some choice about what he or she reads, but participate in reading discussion—sharing thoughts, ideas, and opinions.
- Allow your child to reread things he or she enjoyed reading previously.
- Allow your child to stop reading something that is not keeping his or her interest.

Parents Take Note

Tips & Tricks to Encourage Reading

Being a successful reader is a predictor for future success as a working adult.

Help your adolescent increase his or her chances of success in high school and beyond by building a family of readers.

How to encourage an adolescent to read:

- Make regular visits to the public library and bookstores/sales.
- Encourage your child to have reading material with him or her wherever he or she goes.
- Read aloud and discuss what you think before, during, and after reading an interesting passage from newspapers, magazines, Web sites, books, and other reading material.
- Help your child build a home library—a bookshelf containing fiction and nonfiction of personal interest.
- Encourage your child to read, or read together, at least 15 minutes every day.
- Allow your child to have some choice about what he or she reads, but participate in reading discussion—sharing thoughts, ideas, and opinions.
- Allow your child to reread things he or she enjoyed reading previously.
- Allow your child to stop reading something that is not keeping his or her interest.

From *SSR with Intervention: A School Library Action Research Project* by Leslie B. Preddy. Westport, CT: Libraries Unlimited. Copyright © 2007.

Parents Take Note

Tips & Tricks to Encourage Reading

Being a successful reader is a predictor for future success as a working adult.

Help your adolescent increase his or her chances of success in high school and beyond by building a family of readers.

How to encourage an adolescent to read:

- Make regular visits to the public library and bookstores/sales.
- Encourage your child to have reading material with him or her wherever he or she goes.
- Read aloud and discuss what you think before, during, and after reading an interesting passage from newspapers, magazines, Web sites, books, and other reading material.
- Help your child build a home library—a bookshelf containing fiction and nonfiction of personal interest.
- Encourage your child to read, or read together, at least 15 minutes every day.
- Allow your child to have some choice about what he or she reads, but participate in reading discussion—sharing thoughts, ideas, and opinions.
- Allow your child to reread things he or she enjoyed reading previously.
- Allow your child to stop reading something that is not keeping his or her interest.

From *SSR with Intervention: A School Library Action Research Project* by Leslie B. Preddy. Westport, CT: Libraries Unlimited. Copyright © 2007.

Readers Take Note

Fiction Reading Strategies

BEFORE Reading
- Predict what the story might be about based on the cover and title.
- Read the back cover or inside of jacket flap and think about how it might connect to your life or world.

DURING Reading
- Make pictures in your mind—visualize what you are reading.
- Find content clues to help you figure out unfamiliar words.
- Reread a section that is confusing to you.
- Does your reading raise a question? Search for the answer as you continue to read.
- What language (or words) does the author use to set the mood or tone in your mind?

AFTER Reading
- What was easy about what you read? What was hard?
- Is there a theme or moral?
- How does what you read relate to your life? Your community? The world?
- How does what you read relate to other things you've read?
- What fix-up strategies were helpful for making sense of the reading?

Readers Take Note

Fiction Reading Strategies

BEFORE Reading
- Predict what the story might be about based on the cover and title.
- Read the back cover or inside of jacket flap and think about how it might connect to your life or world.

DURING Reading
- Make pictures in your mind—visualize what you are reading.
- Find content clues to help you figure out unfamiliar words.
- Reread a section that is confusing to you.
- Does your reading raise a question? Search for the answer as you continue to read.
- What language (or words) does the author use to set the mood or tone in your mind?

AFTER Reading
- What was easy about what you read? What was hard?
- Is there a theme or moral?
- How does what you read relate to your life? Your community? The world?
- How does what you read relate to other things you've read?
- What fix-up strategies were helpful for making sense of the reading?

From *SSR with Intervention: A School Library Action Research Project* by Leslie B. Preddy. Westport, CT: Libraries Unlimited. Copyright © 2007.

Readers Take Note

Fiction Reading Strategies

BEFORE Reading
- Predict what the story might be about based on the cover and title.
- Read the back cover or inside of jacket flap and think about how it might connect to your life or world.

DURING Reading
- Make pictures in your mind—visualize what you are reading.
- Find content clues to help you figure out unfamiliar words.
- Reread a section that is confusing to you.
- Does your reading raise a question? Search for the answer as you continue to read.
- What language (or words) does the author use to set the mood or tone in your mind?

AFTER Reading
- What was easy about what you read? What was hard?
- Is there a theme or moral?
- How does what you read relate to your life? Your community? The world?
- How does what you read relate to other things you've read?
- What fix-up strategies were helpful for making sense of the reading?

From *SSR with Intervention: A School Library Action Research Project* by Leslie B. Preddy. Westport, CT: Libraries Unlimited. Copyright © 2007.

Readers Take Note

Factual/Informational Text Reading Strategies

BEFORE Reading
- What is your purpose for reading this? What do you want to know? To learn?
- What do you already know about this topic?
- Skim and Scan—look at the contents page, words in bold, words in italic, pictures and their captions, and text boxes.

DURING Reading
- Look at pictures and their captions.
- Make pictures in your mind—visualize what you are reading.
- Find content clues to help you figure out unfamiliar words.
- Reread a section that confuses you.
- Does your reading raise a question? Search for the answer as you continue to read.

AFTER Reading
- Retell what you just read.
- Skim and reread to find details to answer your questions.
- How did your understanding and meaning change after reading?
- What was easy about what you read? What was hard?
- How does what you read relate to your life? Your community? The world?
- How does what you read relate to other things you've read?
- What fix-up strategies were helpful for making sense of the reading?

From *SSR with Intervention: A School Library Action Research Project* by Leslie B. Preddy. Westport, CT: Libraries Unlimited. Copyright © 2007.

Readers Take Note

Factual/Informational Text Reading Strategies

BEFORE Reading
- What is your purpose for reading this? What do you want to know? To learn?
- What do you already know about this topic?
- Skim and Scan—look at the contents page, words in bold, words in italic, pictures and their captions, and text boxes.

DURING Reading
- Look at pictures and their captions.
- Make pictures in your mind—visualize what you are reading.
- Find content clues to help you figure out unfamiliar words.
- Reread a section that confuses you.
- Does your reading raise a question? Search for the answer as you continue to read.

AFTER Reading
- Retell what you just read.
- Skim and reread to find details to answer your questions.
- How did your understanding and meaning change after reading?
- What was easy about what you read? What was hard?
- How does what you read relate to your life? Your community? The world?
- How does what you read relate to other things you've read?
- What fix-up strategies were helpful for making sense of the reading?

From *SSR with Intervention: A School Library Action Research Project* by Leslie B. Preddy. Westport, CT: Libraries Unlimited. Copyright © 2007.

Readers Take Note

Factual/Informational Text Reading Strategies

BEFORE Reading
- What is your purpose for reading this? What do you want to know? To learn?
- What do you already know about this topic?
- Skim and Scan—look at the contents page, words in bold, words in italic, pictures and their captions, and text boxes.

DURING Reading
- Look at pictures and their captions.
- Make pictures in your mind—visualize what you are reading.
- Find content clues to help you figure out unfamiliar words.
- Reread a section that confuses you.
- Does your reading raise a question? Search for the answer as you continue to read.

AFTER Reading
- Retell what you just read.
- Skim and reread to find details to answer your questions.
- How did your understanding and meaning change after reading?
- What was easy about what you read? What was hard?
- How does what you read relate to your life? Your community? The world?
- How does what you read relate to other things you've read?
- What fix-up strategies were helpful for making sense of the reading?

From *SSR with Intervention: A School Library Action Research Project* by Leslie B. Preddy. Westport, CT: Libraries Unlimited. Copyright © 2007.

Readers Take Note

What Might I Like to Read?
Good Questions to Ask Myself

What type of novel or nonfiction might you enjoy?

Use these questions to help yourself narrow your focus.

- What games do I like to play?
- What do I like to do in my free time?
- What are my hobbies?
- What sports do I like to watch or play?
- What TV shows do I like to watch?
- What movies do I like to see?
- What is my favorite subject in school?
- What is my favorite family event or story?
- What do I like to do with family?
- What do I like to do with friends?
- What is my favorite book? Who wrote it?
- What authors have I read before and liked?
- What type (genre) of book have I read before and enjoyed?
- Ask trusted friends what they like to read.

Still not sure what to read?

Share some of your answers with your library media specialist or classroom teacher for help.

From *SSR with Intervention: A School Library Action Research Project* by Leslie B. Preddy. Westport, CT: Libraries Unlimited. Copyright © 2007.

Readers Take Note

What Might I Like to Read?
Good Questions to Ask Myself

What type of novel or nonfiction might you enjoy?

Use these questions to help yourself narrow your focus.

- What games do I like to play?
- What do I like to do in my free time?
- What are my hobbies?
- What sports do I like to watch or play?
- What TV shows do I like to watch?
- What movies do I like to see?
- What is my favorite subject in school?
- What is my favorite family event or story?
- What do I like to do with family?
- What do I like to do with friends?
- What is my favorite book? Who wrote it?
- What authors have I read before and liked?
- What type (genre) of book have I read before and enjoyed?
- Ask trusted friends what they like to read.

Still not sure what to read?

Share some of your answers with your library media specialist or classroom teacher for help.

From *SSR with Intervention: A School Library Action Research Project* by Leslie B. Preddy. Westport, CT: Libraries Unlimited. Copyright © 2007.

Readers Take Note

What Might I Like to Read?
Good Questions to Ask Myself

What type of novel or nonfiction might you enjoy?

Use these questions to help yourself narrow your focus.

- What games do I like to play?
- What do I like to do in my free time?
- What are my hobbies?
- What sports do I like to watch or play?
- What TV shows do I like to watch?
- What movies do I like to see?
- What is my favorite subject in school?
- What is my favorite family event or story?
- What do I like to do with family?
- What do I like to do with friends?
- What is my favorite book? Who wrote it?
- What authors have I read before and liked?
- What type (genre) of book have I read before and enjoyed?
- Ask trusted friends what they like to read.

Still not sure what to read?

Share some of your answers with your library media specialist or classroom teacher for help.

From *SSR with Intervention: A School Library Action Research Project* by Leslie B. Preddy. Westport, CT: Libraries Unlimited. Copyright © 2007.

Readers Take Note

Is This Reading for You?

The Official "Five Finger Rule"

Place your hand on the table. Open to a page and begin reading. Put one finger down for every word read that you don't know and can't figure out through clues in the text. If you have all five fingers on the table before you finished reading the page, it may be too hard. Try setting it aside and find something different

The Official "Three Chapter Rule"

Sometimes it takes time to get into the flow of a good book, but if you don't get it or feel it will be worth your time after two chapters, give it one more chapter. Not every book is for every person. If after chapter three, you still aren't interested, stop reading it and start something new.

The Official "Repeat It Rule"

Read a page, then set it down. Can you retell most of what you just read? If not, try something else.

From *SSR with Intervention: A School Library Action Research Project* by Leslie B. Preddy. Westport, CT: Libraries Unlimited. Copyright © 2007.

Readers Take Note

Is This Reading for You?

The Official "Five Finger Rule"

Place your hand on the table. Open to a page and begin reading. Put one finger down for every word read that you don't know and can't figure out through clues in the text. If you have all five fingers on the table before you finished reading the page, it may be too hard. Try setting it aside and find something different

The Official "Three Chapter Rule"

Sometimes it takes time to get into the flow of a good book, but if you don't get it or feel it will be worth your time after two chapters, give it one more chapter. Not every book is for every person. If after chapter three, you still aren't interested, stop reading it and start something new.

The Official "Repeat It Rule"

Read a page, then set it down. Can you retell most of what you just read? If not, try something else.

From *SSR with Intervention: A School Library Action Research Project* by Leslie B. Preddy. Westport, CT: Libraries Unlimited. Copyright © 2007.

Readers Take Note

Is This Reading for You?

The Official "Five Finger Rule"

Place your hand on the table. Open to a page and begin reading. Put one finger down for every word read that you don't know and can't figure out through clues in the text. If you have all five fingers on the table before you finished reading the page, it may be too hard. Try setting it aside and find something different

The Official "Three Chapter Rule"

Sometimes it takes time to get into the flow of a good book, but if you don't get it or feel it will be worth your time after two chapters, give it one more chapter. Not every book is for every person. If after chapter three, you still aren't interested, stop reading it and start something new.

The Official "Repeat It Rule"

Read a page, then set it down. Can you retell most of what you just read? If not, try something else.

From *SSR with Intervention: A School Library Action Research Project* by Leslie B. Preddy. Westport, CT: Libraries Unlimited. Copyright © 2007.

Readers Take Note
Words to Know

New Word: _____

Based on context clues, I think it means . . .

The Dictionary says it means . . .

New Word: _____

Based on context clues, I think it means . . .

The Dictionary says it means . . .

New Word: _____

Based on context clues, I think it means . . .

The Dictionary says it means . . .

Readers Take Note
Words to Know

New Word: _____

Based on context clues, I think it means . . .

The Dictionary says it means . . .

New Word: _____

Based on context clues, I think it means . . .

The Dictionary says it means . . .

New Word: _____

Based on context clues, I think it means . . .

The Dictionary says it means . . .

Readers Take Note
Words to Know

New Word: _____

Based on context clues, I think it means . . .

The Dictionary says it means . . .

New Word: _____

Based on context clues, I think it means . . .

The Dictionary says it means . . .

New Word: _____

Based on context clues, I think it means . . .

The Dictionary says it means . . .

Readers Take Note

Rate the Read

Title: _____

Author: _____

Genre: _____

Score

1   2   3   4   5   6

Title: _____

Author: _____

Genre: _____

Score

1   2   3   4   5   6

Title: _____

Author: _____

Genre: _____

Score

1   2   3   4   5   6

Title: _____

Author: _____

Genre: _____

Score

1   2   3   4   5   6

Readers Take Note

Rate the Read

Title: _____

Author: _____

Genre: _____

Score

1   2   3   4   5   6

Title: _____

Author: _____

Genre: _____

Score

1   2   3   4   5   6

Title: _____

Author: _____

Genre: _____

Score

1   2   3   4   5   6

Title: _____

Author: _____

Genre: _____

Score

1   2   3   4   5   6

Readers Take Note

Rate the Read

Title: _____

Author: _____

Genre: _____

Score

1   2   3   4   5   6

Title: _____

Author: _____

Genre: _____

Score

1   2   3   4   5   6

Title: _____

Author: _____

Genre: _____

Score

1   2   3   4   5   6

Title: _____

Author: _____

Genre: _____

Score

1   2   3   4   5   6

Readers Take Note

Wish List–Things to Read

- Title: _____
  Author: _____
  Call Number: _____

- Title: _____
  Author: _____
  Call Number: _____

- Title: _____
  Author: _____
  Call Number: _____

- Title: _____
  Author: _____
  Call Number: _____

- Title: _____
  Author: _____
  Call Number: _____

- Title: _____
  Author: _____
  Call Number: _____

Readers Take Note

Wish List–Things to Read

- Title: _____
  Author: _____
  Call Number: _____

- Title: _____
  Author: _____
  Call Number: _____

- Title: _____
  Author: _____
  Call Number: _____

- Title: _____
  Author: _____
  Call Number: _____

- Title: _____
  Author: _____
  Call Number: _____

- Title: _____
  Author: _____
  Call Number: _____

Readers Take Note

Wish List–Things to Read

- Title: _____
  Author: _____
  Call Number: _____

- Title: _____
  Author: _____
  Call Number: _____

- Title: _____
  Author: _____
  Call Number: _____

- Title: _____
  Author: _____
  Call Number: _____

- Title: _____
  Author: _____
  Call Number: _____

- Title: _____
  Author: _____
  Call Number: _____

Bibliography

ACT. "Reading between the Lines: What the ACT Reveals about College Readiness in Reading." 2006. http://www.act.org/path/policy/reports/reading.html. (Accessed 6 June 2006).

American Library Association. "Booktalking." 2006. http://www.ala.org/ala/yalsa/profdev/booktalking.htm. (Accessed 1 June 2006).

Birkerts, Sven. "The Secret Life of Children: Learning How to Read Nourishes a Child's Sense of Self in Ways We Cannot Begin to Imagine." *School Library Journal* 45 (9): 141–143 (1999).

Bishop, Kay. *Connecting Libraries with Classrooms: The Curricular Roles of the Media Specialist.* Washington, OH: Linworth, 2003.

Burke, Jim. *Reading Reminders: Tools, Tips, and Techniques.* Portsmouth, NH: Heinemann, 2000.

Callison, Daniel, and Leslie Preddy. *The Blue Book on Information Age Inquiry, Instruction and Literacy.* Westport, CT: Libraries Unlimited, 2006.

Cornwell, Linda, and Julie Gillespie. "Reading Comprehension: The Bridge to Information Literacy." Workshop presentation at Scholastic Literacy Workshop, Indianapolis, IN, January 2004.

Curtis, Mary E., and Ann Marie Longo. *When Adolescents Can't Read: Methods and Materials That Work.* Newton, MA: Brookline Books, 1999.

Donham, Jean. *Enhancing Teaching and Learning: A Leadership Guide for School Library Media Specialists.* New York: Neal-Schuman, 1998.

Dreher, Mariam Jean. "Motivating Teachers to Read." *The Reading Teacher* 56 (4): 338–340 (2002/2003).

Ellsberry, Jim. "Twenty-One Teaching Methods for the Analogical Teacher's Classroom." Workshop presentation at the Metropolitan School District of Perry Township DeWitt Institute for Professional Development Seminar, Indianapolis, IN, July 1998.

Everhart, Nancy. "Accelerated Reader." American Library Association. 2005. http://www.ala.org/ala/aasl/aaslpubsandjournals/slmrb/slmrcontents/volume82005/reader.htm. (Accessed 6 February 2006).

Fountas, Irene C., and Gay Su Pinnell. *Guiding Readers and Writers: Teaching Comprehension, Genre, and Content Literacy.* Portsmouth, NH: Heinemann, 2001.

Gardiner, Steve. "A Skill for Life." *Educational Leadership* 63 (2): 67–70 (2005).

Harste, Jerome C., et al. *Creating Classrooms for Authors and Inquirers.* 2nd ed. Portsmouth, NH: Heinemann, 1996.

Haycock, Ken. "Collaborative Literature-Based Reading Programs with Motivation Components." *Teacher Librarian* 33 (2): 38 (2005).

———. *Foundations for Effective School Library Media Programs.* Englewood, CO: Libraries Unlimited, 1999.

Holland, Earlene, and Jack W. Humphrey. "Study of Reading in Indiana Middle, Junior, and Senior High Schools." Middle Grades Reading Network. March 2004. http://mgrn.evansville.edu/study2004.htm. (Accessed 25 March 2006).

Horton, Rosemary. "Boys Are People Too: Boys and Reading, Truth and Misconceptions." *Teacher Librarian* 33 (2): 30–32 (2005).

Indiana Department of Education. "Indiana Accountability System for Academic Progress (ASAP)." 2005. http://www.doe.state.in.us/asap/welcome.html. (Accessed 30 March 2006).

———. "ISTEP+ InfoCenter." 2005. http://www.doe.state.in.us/istep/2005/welcome.html. (Accessed 2 April 2006).

———. "Statewide ISTEP+ Results Show Gains in Math; Modest Improvements in English/Language Arts and Science." News Release. 22 December 2005. http://www.doe.state.in.us/reed/newsr/2005/12-December/ISTEPresults.html. (Accessed 2 April 2006).

Indiana Library Federation-Association for Indiana Media Educators. "Read Aloud Books Too Good to Miss." http://ilfonline.org/AIME/ReadAloud/ReadAloud.htm. (Accessed 7 July 2006).

Johnston, Tony. *That Summer.* Illustrated by Barry Moser. San Diego, CA: Harcourt, 2002.

Kramer, Bill. "What Motivates Students to Read?," *Indiana Reading Journal* 34 (3): 22–29 (2002).

Krashen, Stephen. "Accelerated Reader: Evidence Still Lacking." *Knowledge Quest* 33 (3): 48–49 (2005).

———. "Is In-School Free Reading Good for Children? Why the National Reading Panel Is (Still) Wrong." *Phi Delta Kappan* 86 (6): 444–447 (2005).

———. "More Smoke and Mirrors: A Critique of the National Reading Panel (NRP) Report on 'Fluency.'" *Phi Delta Kappan* 83 (3): 119–123 (2001).

———. *The Power of Reading: Insights from the Research.* 2d ed. Westport, CT: Libraries Unlimited, 2004.

———, and Jeff McQuillan. *The Case for Late Intervention: Once a Good Reader, Always a Good Reader.* Culver City, CA: Language Education Associates, 1996.

Lance, Keith Curry. "Powering Achievement: The Latest Evidence on How School Libraries Matter to Academic Achievement." Presentation at American Association of School Librarians Annual Conference, Kansas City, MO, October 2003.

Langemack, Chapple. *The Booktalker's Bible: How to Talk about Books You Love to Any Audience.* Westport, CT: Libraries Unlimited, 2003.

Libraries and Reading: Indispensable Partners. Evansville, IN: Middle Grades Reading Network, 1996.

McGann, Mary. "Brain Matters Preview." Workshop presentation at Metropolitan School District of Perry Township Professional Development Seminar, Indianapolis, IN, May 2003.

McKenzie, Jamie. "Power Reading and the School Library." *Library Media Connection* 23 (5): 14–19 (2005).

Milam, Peggy. "Scientifically Based Reading Research: Implications for Instruction." *School Library Media Activities Monthly* 20 (2): 20–22, 26 (2003).

Millikan, Ann. "Read Naturally Strategy: Fluency and Comprehension." Presentation at Indiana State Reading Association Annual Conference, Indianapolis, IN, March 2003.

Montiel-Overall, Patricia. "Theory." American Library Association. 2005. http://www.ala.org/ala/aasl/aaslpubsandjournals/slmrb/slmrcontents/volume82005/theory.htm. (Accessed 28 February 2006).

Moore, David W., et al. "Adolescent Literacy: A Position Paper for the Commission on Adolscent Literacy of the International Reading Association." International Reading Association, 1999. http://www.reading.org/downloads/positions/ps1036_adolescent.pdf. (Accessed 1 June 2006).

National Endowment for the Arts. "Reading at Risk: A Survey of Literary Reading in America." Research Division Report #46. 2004. http://www.nea.gov/pub/ReadingAtRisk.pdf. (Accessed 1 June 2006).

National Reading Panel. "Teaching Children to Read: An Evidence-Based Assessment of the Scientific Research Literature on Reading and Its Implications for Reading Instruction." NIH Publication No. 00-4754. 2000. http://www.nichd.nih.gov/publications/nrp/report.htm. (Accessed 1 February 2006).

Olson, Carol Booth. *The Reading/Writing Connection: Strategies for Teaching and Learning in the Secondary Classroom.* Boston: Allyn and Bacon, 2003.

Ontario Library Association. "School Libraries & Student Achievement in Ontario." 2006. http://www.accessola.com/osla/graphics/eqao_pfe_study_2006.pdf. (Accessed 1 June 2006).

Perlstein, Linda. *Not Much Just Chillin': The Hidden Lives of Middle Schoolers.* New York: Farrar, Straus and Giroux, 2003.

Plucker, Jonathan A., et al. *Improving School Libraries and Independent Reading: 1997–2002 Impact Evaluation of the K–12 School Library Printed Materials Grant.* Policy Issue Report #2002–02. Bloomington: Indiana University-Indiana Education Policy Center, 2002.

"Poll Says Most Teens Value Reading." *School Library Journal* 47 (8): 16 (2001).

Reading: An Indispensable Subject for All Middle Grade Students. Evansville, IN: Middle Grades Reading Network, 1996.

Research Foundation Paper: School Libraries Work! 2006 ed. Danbury, CT: Scholastic Library Publishing. 2006. http://www.scholastic.com/librarians/printables/downloads/slw_2006.pdf. (Accessed 6 December 2006).

Robb, Laura. "Reading Strategies That Work." Presentation at the Adolescent Literacy Conference, Indianapolis, IN, June 2005.

————. *Teaching Reading in Middle School.* New York: Scholastic, 2000.

Rosen, Michael. *Michael Rosen's Sad Book.* Illustrated by Quentin Blake. Cambridge, MA: Candlewick, 2004.

"School Improvement Plan: NCA/P.L. 221/NCLBA." Perry Meridian Middle School. 1 May 2005.

"School Improvement Plan: NCA/P.L. 221/NCLBA." Perry Meridian Middle School. 1 May 2006."

Shin, Fay. "Should We Just Tell Them to Read? The Role of Direct Encouragement in Promoting Recreational Reading." *Knowledge Quest* 32 (3): 47–48 (2005).

Short, Kathy G., et al. *Creating Classrooms for Authors and Inquirers.* 2nd ed. Portsmouth, NH: Heinemann, 1996.

Smith, Frank. *Joining the Literacy Club.* Portsmouth, NH: Heinneman, 1988.

Smith, Michael W., and Jeffrey D. Wilhelm. *"Reading Don't Fix No Chevys": Literacy in the Lives of Young Men.* Portsmouth, NH: Heinemann, 2002.

Staton, Maria. "Reading Motivation: The Librarian's Role in Helping Teachers Develop Programs That Work." *Library Talk* 11 (4): 18–20 (1998).

Stripling, Barbara K., and Sandra Hughes-Hassell. *Curriculum Connections: Through the Library.* Westport, CT: Libraries Unlimited, 2003.

Tovani, Cris. *Do I Really Have to Teach Reading? Content Comprehension, Grades 6–12.* Portland, ME: Stenhouse, 2004.

————. "The Power of Purposeful Reading." *Educational Leadership* 63 (2): 48–51 (2005).

Wolfe, Patricia. "Brain Matters: Translating Research into Classroom Practice." Workshop presentation at Metropolitan School District of Perry Township Professional Development Seminar, Indianapolis, IN, June 2003.

Zimmerman, Nancy. "Research-Based Evidence: The Role of the Library Media Specialist in Reading Comprehension Instruction." *School Library Media Activities Monthly* 21 (9): 47–50 (2005).

Index

About the Author

LESLIE B. PREDDY is the LMS at Perry Meridian Middle School in Indianapolis. She has been active in the AASL is an adjunct professor at IUPUI and is co-author with Dr. Danny Callison on *The Blue Book on Information Age Inquiry, Instruction and Literacy* (Libraries Unlimited, 2006).